T0115341

Advance Praise for
The Last Gold Rush... Ever!

"Timing is everything in finance, and Charles Goyette and Bill Haynes have nailed it, releasing an authoritative book on gold just as an epic bull market in precious metals gains traction. As the authors correctly predict, 'The new bull market will take gold to never-before-seen levels—perhaps even to unimaginable new heights where trying to measure the price of gold in dollars becomes quite pointless.'"

—John Rubino, DollarCollapse.com, and co-author of
The Money Bubble: What To Do Before It Pops

"Bestselling author Charles Goyette hits another homerun with his latest book *The Last Gold Rush...Ever!* If you want to know what's in store for the US global military empire and gold, do yourself a favor and read this important book!"

—Michael Shedlock, Global Economic Trend Analysis,
TheStreet.com

"An excellent book, with all the reasons gold is going much higher. Its timing is excellent. As a bonus, it is well-written. I especially liked all the great—and not generally well-known—historical anecdotes."

—Doug Casey, Bestselling Author and Chairman,
Casey Research

"Charles Goyette and Bill Haynes are wise, knowledgeable, and brilliant. If you want to protect your family and yourself in these crazed times, read their book."

—Lew Rockwell, Founder and Chairman,
The Mises Institute, LewRockwell.com

"All fiat currencies eventually die. From the Federal Reserve's money manipulation to the spread of socialism, Charles Goyette and Bill Haynes explain why the dollar is no different. With Uncle Sam now running $3 trillion annual deficits and the Feds hoovering up every dodgy asset in existence, there couldn't be a better time to learn how to protect yourself with gold."

—Mark Nestmann, The Nestmann Group, Ltd.

THE LAST
GOLD RUSH
...EVER!

7 REASONS FOR THE RUNAWAY GOLD MARKET AND HOW YOU CAN PROFIT FROM IT

CHARLES GOYETTE
AND BILL HAYNES

Post Hill
PRESS

A POST HILL PRESS BOOK

ISBN: 978-1-63758-226-8

The Last Gold Rush…Ever!:
7 Reasons for the Runaway Gold Market and How You Can Profit
from It
© 2020 by Charles Goyette and Bill Haynes
All Rights Reserved
First Post Hill Press Hardcover Edition: October 2020

The information and advice herein is not intended to replace the services of financial professionals, with knowledge of your personal financial situation. The advice and strategies contained herein may not be suitable for your situation. You should consult with a professional where appropriate. Neither the publisher nor author shall be liable for any loss of any profit or any other commercial damages, including, but not limited to special, incidental, consequential, or other damages. All investments are subject to risk, which should be considered prior to making any financial decisions.

No part of this book may be reproduced, stored in a retrieval system, or transmitted by any means without the written permission of the author and publisher.

Post Hill Press
New York • Nashville
posthillpress.com
Published in the United States of America

*To Ron Paul
One of the greatest champions of liberty of this age
or any other.*

CONTENTS

FOREWORD
By David A. Stockman

America's now crumbling empire of debt, like Rome itself, was not built in a day.

On October 1, 1982, day one of President Ronald Reagan's first full budget year, I told the House Budget Committee that if fiscal sanity was to prevail, they were doomed to spend the rest of their careers cutting spending. After years of Lyndon Johnson's Great Society and Nixon-Ford welfare programs that sought to outdo LBJ, it fell to me as the director of the Office of Management and Budget to explain the facts of economic life, even—and perhaps especially—to old Washington hands.

"There is no final vote," I warned. "Twenty years of history aren't going to be corrected in twenty weeks."

In fact, as I soon discovered, nothing at all was going to be corrected. That year's deficit broke for the first time into what in the "billion here, billion there" era we called triple-digits: more than $100 billion. In fact, it didn't just break into triple-digit territory. It crashed right through, rolled over a few times, and landed in a ditch. That year, the deficit totaled $128 billion.

The next year, it was $208 billion.

At the same time, the gross national debt surged past a trillion dollars. By the time I left Washington for Wall Street a few years later, I hoped only that catastrophe could be avoided.

But fiscal sanity did not prevail; now, in the brave new world of $3 trillion and $4 trillion deficits, America is being turned into a coast-to-coast soup line.

But of course, the debt couldn't have grown to such gargantuan proportions in a sound money environment. Nixon's taking the US off the gold standard eleven years earlier was the enabling act for the massive monetary corruption and money-printing spree that would follow at the hands of Keynesian icons at the Federal Reserve: Greenspan, Bernanke, Yellen, and now Powell.

The Last Gold Rush…Ever! aptly identifies these as among the "Deep State Money Manipulators." Under their guidance central banking became the tool of a vicious form of crony capitalism and money politics. So that today the economy has become utterly dependent upon the central bank's printing press, the bipartisan fiscal regime of perma-deficits, and the military-industrial complex that bolsters what remains of the manufacturing sector.

Now, in their hideous series of bubbles and busts—the dot-com bubble and the housing bubble among them, each one bigger than the last—the stock market bubble has burst, leaving the stench of catastrophe hanging heavy in the air.

There were plenty of other pins that might have done the job. Another needless Washington war, for example, could have done as much. But it happened that COVID-19 was the pin that popped the Wall Street bubble.

Just as I learned that the book now in your hands was forthcoming, the clamor to participate in the plunder triggered by Wall Street's sell-off and the general lockdown reached a fevered pitch. With years of state cronyism, bankster bailouts, and special pleading assimilated into our national ethos, lines of supplicants began forming around the whited palaces of DC, their eyes beady and greedy, their sweaty palms extended to grab their share. They had all learned never to let a good crisis go to waste.

The beggars in line on Capitol Hill weren't the homeless by any means. They were some of the biggest corporations in America, making the failed but ever-ready Keynesian claim that budgetary red ink somehow would be stimulative.

Among those at the head of the handout line were the nation's airlines. Notoriously cyclical and vulnerable to dislocations caused by recessions, storms, wars, and terror, they had failed to prepare for well-known risks. Instead, the airline industry spent decades strip-mining their balance sheets to fund share buybacks and goose top executive stock options when they should have been preparing to protect their companies. Since 2012, management of the four largest US airlines—Delta, United, American, and Southwest—spent $43.7 billion on share buybacks to enrich themselves and their shareholders. Then, when their flights hit an air pocket, they turned to the taxpayers to provide them $50 billion in bailouts that the they couldn't bother to provide for themselves.

Who hasn't learned from such examples? So this time, even tennis shoe sellers, beer brewers, and candymakers pressed their claims on the public purse. If you looked closely you probably would have seen the butchers, the bakers, and the candlestick makers too.

At the Eccles Building on Constitution Avenue, the Federal Reserve announced special provisions galore for the banks that had created it in the first place. Changes in reserve requirements, more liquidity provisions, and anything else that would help bail out the stock market were rolled into the Powell burrito. It would, announced a magnanimous Fed, print whatever money it took (using "its full range of tools," as the statement read). So, the Fed stepped up to the plate to buy more government bonds, hundreds of billions of dollars' worth with each swing of the bat. And not just government bonds, but mortgage and other asset-backed securities, as well as corporate and municipal securities.

At the same time, it extended new credit facilities to foreign central banks far and wide: $60 billion each to the central banks of Australia, Brazil, Korea, Mexico, Singapore, and Sweden, and $30 billion to those of Denmark, Norway, and New Zealand. Those were in addition to the preexisting credit arrangements it provides to the Bank of Canada, the Bank of England, the Bank of Japan, the European Central Bank, and the Swiss National Bank. By the way, at least three of those countries have higher per capita incomes than the US.

Meanwhile, at the White House, they were talking about the marriage of corporations and the state. Asked if he liked the idea of the government taking stock in private companies, president Donald Trump answered with the words of a wedding vow. "I do. I really do," he said. It's a union Mussolini could have officiated.

On the White House lawn, the administration was warming up the helicopters of monetarist lore to drop wads of cash directly into the accounts of the people. Of course, that had to be a part of the plan this time around. Frédéric Bastiat provided the taxonomy of plunder a long time ago: The few plunder the many; or, everybody plunders everybody; or, nobody plunders anybody.

Nobody plunders anybody doesn't stand a chance. And while the few plunder the many has been the Washington way, growing resentment of the 1 percent, Occupy Wall Street, Antifa violence, and the energized socialists Sanders, Warren, and Ocasio-Cortez mean fresh plunder initiatives have to provide Free Stuff for everybody. If the Fed can print money for Wall Street, it had damn well better be ready to print some for everybody next time. ("Sure, throw them a scrap," say the cronies, knowing full well that in the financial casino the odds always favor the house and that it's worth a few crumbs just to keep the rubes at the table.) The socialist warriors' fondest hope for a windfall notwithstanding, "helicopter money" is only the next economically imbecilic step along the pathway of the Bush-Bernanke bailouts that Bastiat foretold: the plunder of everybody by everybody, an endgame provision that launches a war of all against all.

The Last Gold Rush...Ever! provides the essential orientation you need for the endgame upon which we have embarked. Washington and the Fed are in the process of putting the coup d' grace on capitalism and sound money, so if you are to be prepared to protect yourself and your family, nothing could be more timely than this book.

One more thing. Authors Charles Goyette and Bill Haynes have detailed how Keynesian central banking has poured the kerosene that ignites the debt inferno. But they don't stop there. They describe a series of accelerants—trade and currency wars, a war on cash, a new Washington enthusiasm for the deprivations of socialism, waning worldwide dollar hegemony, and the demise of America's global military empire—that will make this bonfire of calamites burn hotter, the dollar lose value faster, and the gold price race higher than those who fail to read this book might ever suspect.

INTRODUCTION

THE CROSSROADS OF HISTORY

When Everything Happens at Once

*T*he *Last Gold Rush…Ever* is about a different kind of gold rush. It doesn't involve the discovery of a new mother lode like the famous 1849 California Gold Rush. Perhaps the discovery of major terrestrial deposits in remote locations like the Antarctic or technologies that will allow the recovery of oceanic gold or gold from heretofore played-out mines will trigger a rush of that type again. Space mining ventures may someday even set off a race to recover precious metals and other resources from asteroids.

But *The Last Gold Rush…Ever* isn't about prospecting and mining. It is about financial events that occur at the crossroads of history. When a new global reality topples an old financial order. When the State's debts can't be serviced. When the people realize they can't trust the monetary system.

The Last Gold Rush…Ever is about a contagion of capsizing, game-changing events in our fragile economic environment. It is about the economic volatility and the blow-off market we can expect at the end of a currency's life.

Few realize that today's US dollar is the third iteration of the country's currency in less than a hundred years. (It is no consolation that other countries have done worse. Between 1986 and 1994, Brazil had five different currencies.) Since 1933, the US has gone from the gold dollar standard to the gold-exchange dollar standard and finally to the mere dollar standard, the weakest of the three. Now, this dollar standard faces a new era of monetary and geopolitical challenges that it cannot withstand.

When a monetary unit is dying, people scramble to convert their currency into something reliable. Something enduring. Like gold. Tellingly, major world central banks, like Russia's and China's, are leading the movement by converting their dollar reserves to gold. Since the Great Recession, China has more than tripled its gold reserves, while Russia's holdings have quadrupled. They know that gold has monetary virtues that have survived wars and weathered financial storms. Gold has outlasted every conceivable kind of monetary scheme and type of government.

So great are gold's monetary qualities that, as the economist Ludwig von Mises observed, States have had to resort to the most extreme measures, ignoring laws, trampling on their own constitutions, and even resorting to imprisonment and executions to prevail in the competition between their own money and gold.

When the people conclude that their monetary system is subject to endless State manipulation and the rising cost of living isn't just some inexplicable astrological phenomenon, but rather the result of a deliberate debasement of the currency that is likely to continue, they become anxious at first—and eventually desperate—to exchange their hollowed-out currency for gold. They will do so despite even the most punitive laws that forbid them. Such is gold's timeless appeal.

Confrontations between a State's money and gold have occurred time and again throughout history. The flight into real goods—preeminently gold—that happens in a monetary crisis has been lately on display for all to see in Venezuela. It is reenacting a pattern that Mises gave the evocative name "the Crack-Up Boom":

> A breakdown occurs. The crack-up boom appears. Everybody is anxious to swap his money against 'real' goods, no matter whether he needs them or not, no matter how much money he has to pay for them. Within a very short time, within a few weeks or even days, the things which were used as money are no longer used as media of exchange. They become scrap paper. Nobody wants to give away anything against them.

> It was this that happened with the Continental currency in America in 1781, with the French *mandats territoriaux* in 1796, and with the German Mark in 1923. It will happen again whenever the same conditions appear. If a thing has to be used as a medium of exchange, public opinion must not believe that the quantity of this thing will increase beyond all bounds.

While we have seen bull markets in gold in the US—literal gold rushes in the dollar economy in which people have stood in lines around the block to exchange dollars for gold (it happened at the end of the Carter presidency)—so far, the dollar has managed to survive. But like all the world's other irredeemable State paper currencies that have failed, one day there will be a final rush out of the dollar and into gold. As with all the other failed currencies before it, the dollar—at least in its present form—will not survive the event. It will be *The Last Gold Rush…Ever* in the dollar-standard economy.

Three Strikes and You're Out!

There have been three gold bull markets in the last fifty years. President Nixon's repudiation of America's promise to redeem its dollars in gold in 1971 (the end of the gold-exchange dollar standard) led to widespread calamity, including wage and price controls, the Arab oil embargo, and double-digit inflation. A powerful breakout from its long-standing government-controlled price of $35 an ounce, saw gold run up to nearly $200 an ounce in 1974.

That was the first gold bull market of the post-World War II era.

Unfortunately, the lessons that should have been learned by the State's fiscal and monetary authorities from the dislocations and wealth destruction of that first episode were ignored. So before long, with the hapless Carter presidency, it became evident that the dollar was in trouble again, and that it was time for gold and silver to once again take center stage.

Indeed, the period became the highest peacetime inflation in American history; the dollar crisis that had been so inevitable produced another raging and runaway bull market in gold and silver.

Then, during the second bull market, gold marched to $850 an ounce in 1980.

The lessons of that bull market went unlearned as well. As the effects of years of reckless government growth and spending, compounding federal debt, and ruinous interest rate manipulation continued to build, another economic calamity became certain. Ever a barometer of State irresponsibility, gold began stirring again in 2001. Amid bank runs in the fall of 2008, with millions of Americans losing their homes and jobs, and with hundreds of billions of dollars in bank bailouts in the offing, gold was on the march once again.

This third bull market took gold to $1,900 in 2011. Silver's price performance was even more dramatic, just as it had been in the prior bull market. From a low in the fall of 2008 of $9 an ounce, silver surged for the next three years. It had doubled by the beginning of 2010, up to almost $19. By the end of 2010, it was over $30. In 2011 silver closed in on $50 an ounce.

Of course, the lessons of the Great Recession have been ignored by Washington as well. So now, like the gathering of storm clouds, the events that drive bull markets are building on the not-so-distant horizon. Just as each of the prior gold runs was bigger than the one before it, today's economic skies are darker than ever. For reasons we will explain, they threaten a coming monetary calamity much more ominous than any of those that came before.

For the old order of politicians, officials, bureaucrats, their enablers, and those who have proven themselves incapable of learning the age-old lessons of fiscal responsibility and monetary honesty, time has run out.

A terminal event is inevitable.

Not Just Another Bull Market

Deconstructing prior gold bull markets is a useful exercise. A close examination readily distinguishes *The Last Gold Rush… Ever* from merely another secular bull market in gold, one driven primarily by reckless indebtedness and foolhardy money printing.

As important as they are, debt and fiat money (money only because the State says it is money) are but two of seven powerful dynamics at work that justify calling for an endgame event for the US dollar as presently constituted: an unbacked, irredeemable currency issued wantonly without regard to ultimate consequences.

At the Crossroads of History

The new bull market will take gold to never-before-seen levels—perhaps even to unimaginable new heights where trying to measure the price of gold in dollars becomes quite pointless. In fact, the overlapping of just two or three of the seven game-changing developments we describe in *The Last Gold Rush… Ever!* would be enough for a dynamic new gold price move.

Imagine a deepening debt crisis in an environment of stagflation—a period of increasing prices in a low- or no-growth economy—in which the State, ravenous for revenue, unleashes a war on cash and institutes price controls to placate a restive public. Or a military confrontation, a standoff of principals or proxies, driving a couple of Uncle Sam's major creditors to unwind their holdings in US Treasury bonds. The gap would have to be filled by money printing. In fact, the Fed would be forced to be a major bidder in government bond markets to keep foreign dumping of US bonds from tanking the Treasury market and driving interest rates to the moon! And when the Fed bids for assets, it does so by creating money out of "thin air."

But we are not talking about the coincidence of just a couple of game-changing events in the monetary world. We are talking about everything happening at once, a malevolent convergence of seven powerful and mutually reinforcing reasons for *The Last Gold Rush...Ever.*

While any one of these reasons by itself represents an important economic event that can ignite a new and historic collision between gold and State-issued currencies, together they represent the fuel for a bonfire of the Deep State's making.

Just as it has prevailed in similar showdowns throughout time, gold will arise from the ashes of this conflagration.

In *The Last Gold Rush...Ever*, the world's central banks will replace their dollar reserves with gold—a trend that is already well underway. In *The Last Gold Rush...Ever*, foreign nations will no longer fund America's debt and therefore America's foreign wars, as they have been doing. In *The Last Gold Rush... Ever*, units of gold will replace the ever-changing value of the dollar as the benchmark for global business.

In *The Last Gold Rush…Ever*, ordinary, everyday people will cease to measure their wealth in terms of dollars, but will count their wealth by the ounces of gold they own.

That is because gold always prevails at the crossroads of history.

Triangulating

The Last Gold Rush…Ever! is the result of a unique collaboration. We, co-authors Charles Goyette and Bill Haynes, have in common long-standing expertise in gold and silver and their monetary virtues. But we come from different perspectives: Bill with decades of hands-on functioning in the markets, dealing daily with gold and silver buyers, sellers, and traders, and the minute-by-minute, tick-by-tick movement of the market; Charles from commenting and writing about the geopolitics and economics of the dollar and gold from outside the industry.

Coming from different professions with independent perspectives allows us together to assess and triangulate coming events in an unprecedented way. We thought the best way to illustrate the value-added nature of our collaboration and the resulting consensus you will discover, is for each of us to introduce himself.

Charles Goyette

Although I first became involved in the gold markets back in the 1970s, I have spent most of the years since writing and speaking about geopolitics and the economy from outside the industry.

In addition to speaking at major economic and investment conferences across the country, my commentary has included hundreds of radio and television appearances. I have often been called upon to share my views with national televisions audiences, including on Fox News, CNN, MSNBC, PBS, CNBC, and Fox Business Network. In 2013 and 2014, I joined forces with former presidential candidate Congressman Ron Paul on the nationally syndicated radio commentary *Ron Paul's America*, which was heard daily on 125 radio stations.

Amid bank runs in the fall of 2008, with millions of Americans losing their jobs, and with hundreds of billions of dollars in bank bailouts in the offing, I agreed to write a book explaining the events. It focused on the role of precious metals in vibrant economies and sound monetary systems throughout history, and compared gold to "paper" money or (more accurately today) money created out of nothing more than digital bookkeeping entries. It described the causative role in the unfolding calamity of the Federal Reserve System, the never-audited and strangely secretive monetary arm of the Deep State.

The Dollar Meltdown quickly became a *New York Times* bestseller. It recounted the way monetary crises typically unfold; provided instructive precedents about wage and price controls, rationing, and currency restrictions from similar economic dislocations in the past; and described the damage they do to entire countries as well as to unprepared individuals and their families. I wrote that my intention was to prepare readers with a briefing that would prove valuable over time, seeking to arm them "for more than just the investment conditions of this year, the next, and the year after. I have wandered through history, monetary theory, and economic principles to help you recognize syndromes, remember precedents, and be equipped to make sound judgments so you can profit from both the expected and the unexpected, now and in the future."

Today, more than a decade later, is that future. We wrote this book so that readers will not be blindsided by fast-approaching events that, for most people, are unexpected.

Bill Haynes

Following a degree in finance from the University of Colorado and training on Wall Street, I became a stockbroker in Denver. But from the beginning, I had my eyes on gold and silver. As I watched President Nixon's repudiation of America's promise to redeem its dollars in gold in 1971 (the end of the gold-exchange dollar standard) and witnessed the widespread calamity of Nixon's wage and price controls regimes, I understood clearly that monetary challenges were building. At the same time, I recognized the growing uses for silver and that dwindling stockpiles would result in much higher silver prices. The company I founded in response was launched to sell silver bullion to investors.

When Americans regained the right to own gold bullion on January 1, 1975, CMI Gold & Silver Inc. was there, one of the first dealers in the country to recommend buying gold.

Since those beginnings, CMI Gold & Silver Inc. has continued to prosper and is today one of the oldest gold and silver dealers in the US and has played a major role in introducing many thousands of investors to the gold and silver markets.

Today, late in my career, it is my mission to share what I have learned about the markets and the economic and monetary practices that make *The Last Gold Rush...Ever* inevitable.

I think you will find the result of this collaboration to be a valuable guide to protecting yourself and your family and prospering during challenging days ahead.

About This Book

This book is divided into two parts. Part One sets the stage on which *The Last Gold Rush...Ever* is enacted. It discusses first the US dollar and the Federal Reserve that manages it. Next, it examines the compounding debt of the US government. These are the first two of seven reasons for the coming runaway gold market. Due to years of dishonest monetary practices and criminally reckless deficit spending, the fate of the monetary system and the consequences of US debt are not contingent events. The pitiless reckoning of economic law makes them *faits accomplis*: the dollars that have been created have already been created; the debt the government has run up has already been run up. They are both structural realities against which other events must play out.

Part Two addresses those other events. Each one of its five chapters describes something already in motion today, each one casting dark shadows ahead.

While the dollar and debt crises described in Part One are sufficient in themselves for a gold bull market on a hitherto unseen scale, the issues in Part Two can be thought of as accelerants for the last dollar gold bull market. Were it not for the calamity implicit in US monetary and fiscal policy, the rest of these game-changing reasons would not have developed or would not have such destructive power. A war on cash is both unnecessary and unthinkable in an environment of honest money; the socialist experiments that are in place and growing daily could not have been implemented in nation of prudent spending.

All of these seven reasons for *The Last Gold Rush...Ever* are man-made events. They are the consequences of State policies and actions. But always in the background lie other possibilities that are not man-made. These are black swan events: unforeseen, widely unexpected events that can have outsized impact. Among these are natural disasters like cataclysmic earthquakes, plagues, and floods. By definition, these natural-disaster black swans are rare, but they and the economic response to them can topple governments and entire cultures in the blink of an eye, to say nothing of ephemeral State monetary systems.

Finally, in the Epilogue, you will find guidelines for protecting yourself and your family monetarily from such unexpected natural disasters and from the inevitable results of governmental malfeasance. These are specific steps derived from our years of experience with precious metals markets and lifelong studies of similar periods. Mark Twain may not have actually said that history never repeats, but it rhymes. If he didn't say it, he should have, because it is true. While no one can be completely insulated from the crises of a currency breakdown and social disruption, the authoritarian measures and power grabs that accompany them, the dislocations and diminished conditions of many, to say nothing of the prospect of war, it is our hope that you will benefit by anticipating the rhymes of our economic history.

In *The Last Gold Rush...Ever*, many will be impoverished.

Only a few will prosper.

Part One

SETTING THE STAGE

CHAPTER 1

THE DEEP STATE MONEY MANIPULATORS

Hiding in Plain Sight

People have a hard time accepting anything that overwhelms them.

—Bob Dylan

Meet the Deep State

If you've ever wondered why the American people get more wars after they elect a liberal peace-prize candidate...

If you've ever wanted to know why the government gets bigger and the people get loaded with more debt after they elect "small government" conservatives to Congress and the White House...

If you've ever wanted to know why someone like Martha Stewart can be sent to prison for lying to the FBI, even though she wasn't in court or under oath at the time, while the Director

3

of National Intelligence, in sworn testimony, can brazenly lie with impunity to Congress and the people…

If you've ever wondered why the head of the Central Intelligence Agency can share highly classified information for his personal benefit and get nothing more than a wrist slap, while whistleblowers who reveal government lies and corruption are hounded to the ends of the earth…

Then it's time for you to learn about the Deep State.

If you wonder why the American middle class has stalled out while banksters and cronies are bailed out…

If you want to know what the future holds for your well-being and that of your children while the Deep State tramples on the Constitution…

And if you would like to know what the Deep State is doing to America's money and economy so that you can prepare, because runaway government and bankrupting wars are only the tip of the iceberg…

Then you'll want to pay close attention to what follows. You will want to pay close attention even if you haven't wondered about any of these things, because, to adapt Leon Trotsky's comment about war, you may not be interested in the Deep State, but the Deep State is interested in you.

Today, more than ever, the Deep State is in charge. And nothing it does ends up well for you. Or for your prosperity.

You may have noted that billionaires Bill Gates, Warren Buffett, and Jeff Bezos together have more wealth than the bottom half of the US population, more than that of 160 million Americans combined. The financialization of the economy, the repression of interest rates for the benefit of the same bankers who got bailed out, the subsidizing of Wall Street, have all done wonders for the powerful crony classes.

By the beginning of 2020, the capitalization of the US stock market was up more than $23.5 trillion since the last crisis, the Great Recession, ended in 2009. Even so, as economist Andy Xie observed from Shanghai, "US capital formation has stagnated for decades. The outlandish paper wealth is just the same asset at ever higher prices." Because the top 10 percent own three-quarters of the wealth, and since 90 percent of the income growth has gone to the top 1 percent, says Xie, asset inflation increases inequality "by definition."

The policies behind these massive dislocations and monetary interventions are implemented without debate from the people; they are not the result of careful deliberation by the people's elected representatives. They are the policy outcome of private boards and bodies, a top-down, central economic organization of the sort discredited by the Soviets' failed experience. In their current incarnation, they are operations run by bureaucrats few Americans have ever heard of, shielded from public view, and operating in ways, as we have learned from a century of bitter experience, that leave nothing but ruin in their wake. That is why our story begins with the Deep State.

In one guise or another, the Deep State and its Money Manipulators have been in business for a very long time, as an observation made two centuries ago will attest. John C. Calhoun, the seventh vice president of the United States, had returned to the Senate, where, in 1836, he rose to oppose a measure that would be familiar today. He was objecting to an amendment that, along with a huge increase in government patronage and enabling the concealment of manipulations of the monetary system, would also provide public money to private banks at no interest:

> A power has risen up in the government greater than the people themselves, consisting of many, and various, and powerful interests, combined into one mass, and held together by the cohesive power of the vast surplus in the banks. This mighty combination will be opposed to any change; and it is to be feared, that such is its influence, no measure to which it is opposed can become a law, however expedient and necessary; and the public money will remain in their possession, to be disposed of, not as the public interest, but as theirs may dictate.

The term "Deep State" did not exist in Calhoun's time. Although it has been in use in some circles in our time, becoming part of the political debate during the period of Trump's impeachment, the term first broke through in the mainstream media when former Reagan speechwriter and *Wall Street Journal* columnist Peggy Noonan wrote about it in October 2013, three years before Trump's election: "I have come to wonder if we don't have what amounts to a deep state within the outer state in the US—a deep state consisting of our intelligence and security agencies, which are so vast and far-flung in their efforts that they themselves don't fully know who's in charge and what everyone else is doing."

Noonan was writing in response to president Barack Obama's claim that he didn't know that the US government was tapping German chancellor Angela Merkel's phone. Noonan said the whole thing was nuts. "Does the National Security

Agency think Angela Merkel is planning to blow up Times Square? That would be just like her, wouldn't it?"

Noonan's column described her appearance on a CBS *Face the Nation* panel the day before with Philip Shenon, the author of a book on the Kennedy assassination. The show's moderator, Bob Schieffer, observed that government agencies "try to make sure they can't be blamed for something. And, clearly, that is why the FBI and the CIA did not come clean with the Warren Commission."

Schieffer's acknowledgement that the government didn't "come clean" and that the Warren Commission was "one step away from being totally dysfunctional," was fifty years too late. For decades, responsible JFK assassination investigators have been marginalized by media outlets like CBS as "conspiracy theorists" for reporting how elements of the State carefully concealed their activities around the assassination.

Veteran Washington journalist Bob Woodward, also a member of the *Face the Nation* panel that day, connected the discussion to drone strikes and the Obama administration committing assassinations by air. "What's going on here?" Woodward asked. "Who is in control of it? And who can find out?... They need to review this secret world and its power in their government because you run into this rat's nest of concealment and lies time and time again, then and now."

Secret surveillance. Lies. Concealment. Coverups. Assassinations.

Woodward called it a secret world. While others have described it as an invisible or shadow government, Noonan preferred the term Deep State, "the vast, unfathomable and not fully accountable innards of the permanent US intelligence and national security apparatus. I have been wondering if it isn't true that presidents change and directors change—you can keep changing the showbiz side, the names on the marquee—but the ways, needs, demands, imperatives, secrets and strategies of The Agencies stay pretty much the same, except for one thing: They always want more. The dynamic is always toward growth, toward more reach and more power."

More Reach and More Power

The panelists might have thought to mention the role of CIA operatives in the Watergate break-in. Or the indictment of senior CIA, National Security, State, and Defense Department officials in the Iran-Contra crimes. Those with longer memories would have recalled illegal Deep State regime change operations in Iran and Guatemala, as well as the failed Bay of Pigs invasion of Cuba, and many others.

With each passing year it becomes harder for Washington's lapdog press to deny the existence of the Deep State. Many Americans may have missed it when no less a Deep State operative than the Director of National Intelligence, James Clapper, lied under oath to Congress in 2013 in response to the direct question of whether "the NSA collects any type of data at all on millions or hundreds of millions of Americans?"

Clapper answered, "No, sir."

That bald-faced lie, amounting to perjury, was the breaking point for Edward Snowden. It was a last straw, the one that convinced him he had to become a whistleblower and tell the American people what was being done to them. With his breathtaking disclosures, Snowden laid bare the extent of the Deep State's surveillance of the American people.

Denying the existence of the Deep State became implausible.

For his perjury and obstruction of Congress, Clapper went untouched. He remained National Intelligence Director for almost four more years, drawing his $200,000 salary until the end of Obama's administration.

For blowing the whistle on the Deep State, Snowden was charged with violating the Espionage Act of 1917 and had to take sanctuary in Moscow when his passport was canceled. Other countries were threatened to keep them from providing him asylum or safe passage.

With the election of Donald Trump, the curtain was pulled back on some of the means and methods of the Deep State. Senate minority leader Charles Schumer, wise in the ways of Washington, said that Trump was "being really dumb" for taking on the national intelligence community.

"You take on the intelligence community," smirked Schumer, "they have six ways from Sunday of getting back at you."

It was a remark of stunning implications. It made clear the Deep State has and continues to exercise clandestine means of controlling the elected classes and thwarting the decisions of the electorate. They have retaliatory power borne of their spying and data gathering, as well as demonstrable skill at faking evidence if need be, and planting it with the compliant media. Who, then, is in charge if the Deep State has veto power and even potential blackmail power over those the people elect?

It explains why the same policies persist despite the changing majorities and office holders in Washington.

Meet the Money Manipulators

Americans of every political orientation are at last having to confront the Deep State. This is due in part to the torrent of sometimes shocking disclosures from 2016 election hacks and President Trump's complaints about being surveilled. Additionally, an apparent politicization at some level of the FBI, new WikiLeaks discoveries, and the Snowden revelations have continued to call public attention to the reach of the Deep State. Americans are only beginning to discover the permanent and invisible government that operates in its own interests and those of its cronies, regardless of the law or the presidents and parties in power.

They won't have to search far to discover the financial arm of the Deep State. The Federal Reserve System has been hiding in plain sight for more than a hundred years.

This strange, hybrid organization was created by Congress. It presents itself at times as not wholly governmental, at others as not entirely private. It is a peculiar hybrid, considering the Constitution provides for no such entity. But it has proven to be an efficient one for the monetary purposes of the Deep State.

For more than a hundred years, the Federal Reserve has been a serial bubble-blower, inflating the dot-com and housing bubbles. It has quietly overseen the destruction of the dollar's purchasing power. It has stovepiped unimaginable wealth to crony banks and played an essential part in America's growing income inequality. Its interest rate manipulations have encouraged the formation of debt and discouraged capital formation, which is the engine of growth.

The Fed's operations have enabled the continuous expansion of the State and even provided means for the prosecution of the State's undeclared wars. It has secretly provided trillions in loans to private banks and corporations—even to foreign ones. It has vigorously resisted auditing, even as it made "boom and bust" decisions for the entire nation with the sole aim of providing cheap liquidity to the banking cartel that conceived it.

In a corollary to Senator Schumer's warning that a president taking on the Deep State was "being really dumb," and inviting reprisals, one senior Deep State Money Manipulator, William Dudley, a former president of the influential New York Federal Reserve Bank and vice-chairman of the Federal Open Market Committee, caused a firestorm in 2019 when he brazenly encouraged the Fed to sway the next presidential election, writing that the Fed "should consider how their decisions will affect the political outcome in 2020."

Dudley sought to lessen the impact of his comments, but it was an open admission of the Fed's ability to influence political outcomes when it intends to do so. The episode might have shattered illusions for those in the public who believe the Fed operates apolitically. But politicians have long known otherwise.

Richard Nixon saw Fed policies as a cause of his 1960 loss to John Kennedy. The Nixon White House tapes later showed Nixon cajoling and pressuring his appointee, Federal Reserve chairman Arthur Burns, as they repeatedly conferred in 1971 and 1972 about timing Fed interest rate policies to goose the economy in time for Nixon's 1972 reelection. "Time is getting short. We want to get this economy going," said Burns in a phone conversation less than a year before the election.

President Johnson had a more demonstrable way of cajoling people. When the Fed raised interest rates against his wishes,

Johnson summoned Fed chairman William McChesney Martin to his Texas ranch where he berated him and physically shoved him into a wall.

Making Money

Money is half of *every* commercial transaction—from small ones like stopping at Starbucks or paying the neighbor kid to mow your lawn, to the largest ones, such as what you are paid at work or the purchase of your home.

One side is always money. In some cases—when you borrow money or buy insurance—it is both sides.

Maybe it is because it is everywhere that people pay so little attention to what our money is and why it works. In a sense, they are like little children who think milk and eggs come from the grocery store. They don't really give much thought to the whole messy business about cows and chickens at the farm.

In the same way, adults who should know better pay little or no attention to the hidden machinations behind the little green printed pieces of paper and the bookkeeping entries at the bank that account for them. What is forgotten is that paper money, including the dollar, was once merely a claim check or a warehouse receipt for gold or silver that the bank or the treasury was storing on behalf of the noteholder.

The paper dollars were a convenience, but they could be exchanged for the underlying gold or silver at any time. Over the years those State promises were repudiated—in stages—and the people came to believe that paper bills, themselves entirely unredeemable, were the real money. Where the dollars come from and what gives them value are today generally unasked questions.

The answers to all these questions are right in plain sight, which is often the best place to hide.

In fact, one can go through life in America—go through the public schools or even private ones, and watch political debates, national party conventions, and State of the Union addresses—without ever hearing the Federal Reserve System mentioned.

When it is mentioned in schools and by the national media, it is usually with a certain reverence: hushed, soft words of admiration for the "experts" who "regulate" the economy and "solve" our problems. The kid-glove coverage the Fed gets from the media assumes its chairman and its board members are intellectual giants, if not financial deities, who are able to pierce the mysteries of money and economics in a way far beyond the understanding of mere mortals.

But instead of solving problems, the Fed creates them. Because when all the awe and smoke is cleared away, all the Fed really does is manipulate the value of money. And since money is half of every transaction, it is really manipulating everything.

Even things to come.

Gold vs. the State

The Federal Reserve was the Deep State's answer to the world's enduring gold standard. Gold and silver have proven themselves to be superior forms of money for thousands of years. The Babylonians appear to have used gold in a monetary capacity before 2000 BC. An alloy of gold and silver called electrum was used by the world's first mint in Lydia around 700 BC, while King Croesus produced the first pure gold coins there about a century later.

Gold and silver coins share all the characteristics of a dependable money that have been identified since at least the Greek philosopher Aristotle. More than two millennia ago he correctly observed that sound money needs to be durable, portable, divisible, and intrinsically valued or desirable in its own right. Since then, gold coins of the premodern world, coins with familiar names like solidus, bezant, dinar, cruzado, ducat, florin, livre, guilder, and sovereign have served as standards of commerce.

Gold and silver have been so vastly superior that countries with honest precious metals currencies have flourished throughout history, from the marvels of ancient Athens to the Roman republic, the Byzantine empire, Florence of the Renaissance, and the British Empire. The failure of the paper money printed and issued by the Continental Congress ("not worth a Continental" became a figure of speech in the new American republic) was fresh in the mind of the founders of the United States. At the Constitutional Convention in 1787, one delegate said he'd rather reject the entire Constitution than allow the new government to resort to issuing paper money. His disapproval was widely shared by the other delegates. They well understood the history of paper money and specified gold and silver's roles as legal tender in the Constitution.

No paper currency has ever come close to the monetary performance of gold. While gold's performance has shined throughout the ages, the performance of paper money has been accompanied by chaos, collapse, and ruination. Indeed, if you were to ask how many paper currencies have collapsed, instead of tallying up the thousands, a succinct and forward-looking answer might be *all* of them. That is because they don't last. Those that haven't yet failed are only biding their time.

Given a choice between the other things that have been used as money—seashells, cattle, bread, animal skins, chocolate bars, and ordinary pieces of paper with ink—people inevitably prefer the liquidity, dependability, and universal allure of gold.

Never has there been a currency crisis in which people stormed the bank demanding to exchange their gold for paper money.

While people prefer gold, governments do not. Gold imposes a discipline on governments and their spending. The amount of gold in the treasury can't be increased at will or by edict. On the other hand, governments and their central banks can print paper money at will or create its digital equivalent with the keystroke of a computer. Because of the discipline that gold imposes, it is not a surprise to discover that governments are often at war with gold.

Statist economists take great pains to persuade the people that gold has no special value or monetary function. The influential John Maynard Keynes, the advocate of deficit spending and champion of comical monetary policies, called gold a "barbarous relic." Former Federal Reserve chairman Ben Bernanke insisted in congressional testimony that central banks like the Fed only hold gold because it is "a tradition." But hold it they do. In fact, the more militant the State becomes in discrediting gold, determined that gold ownership should not interfere in its monetary schemes, the more insistent it is in keeping all the gold for itself.

One of the earliest experiments with printed money was recorded by the traveler Marco Polo in the thirteenth century. Under penalty of death, the Chinese emperor Kublai Khan forced the acceptance of money printed on mulberry bark, which he could issue in unlimited quantities. As for the gold and silver of China, it unsurprisingly made its way into the Khan's personal vaults.

The revolutionary government of France during the Reign of Terror made it a capital offense for anyone to refuse to accept its paper money, or to distinguish in payment between precious metals and the State's increasingly worthless paper. With gold driven underground, the State's paper-money inflation soared to incredible heights. Soon the paper money was worth less than the paper it was printed on.

Lenin prophesied that after the communist revolution, gold would be used in the construction of public toilets. The reality was quite otherwise. In his chronicle of the Soviet Union's Stalin era, *The Gulag Archipelago*, Alexander Solzhenitsyn quotes Stalin's interrogators and torturers during the Soviet's gold seizures beginning in 1929. Anyone who could have had gold—any jeweler, dental technician, or watch repairman—was suspect. So too was anyone who had a private business, any retailer or craftsman. Anyone who was suspected or denounced as possibly having some gold was rounded up, so the truth or extent of their holdings could be discovered inside prison walls:

Nothing—neither proletarian origin nor revolutionary services—served as a defense against a gold denunciation. All were arrested. All were crammed into GPU cells in numbers no one thought possible up to then—but that was all to the good: they would cough it up all the sooner! It even reached a point of such confusion that men and women were imprisoned in the same cells and used the latrine bucket in each other's presence—who cared about those niceties?... Only one thing was important: Give up your gold, viper! The state needs gold and you don't.

If you had no gold, Solzhenitsyn said, "your situation was hopeless. You would be beaten, burned, tortured, and steamed to the point of death..."

On the other hand, if you had gold and confessed it, it was assumed that you were holding some back, so your suffering continued.

President Franklin Roosevelt unleashed a war on gold in America in 1933 with a nationwide confiscation of the people's gold. Although he had campaigned as a "sound money" candidate, only a month after taking office Roosevelt signed an executive order "forbidding the Hoarding of Gold Coin, Gold Bullion, and Gold Certificates within the continental United States." Roosevelt made sure that the *booboisie*—H. L. Mencken's term for the stupid and gullible of the era—thought that gold hoarders were responsible for the Depression. Foreign devils even played a part in the theft: Roosevelt justified his gold grab under the "Trading with the Enemy Act," a remnant of World War I legislation. The demand to turn private gold over to the government was accompanied by the penalty of a $10,000 fine and ten years of imprisonment.

But many Americans were reading the signs of the times, and the amount of gold coins in circulation and the gold in bank vaults mysteriously began declining steeply months ahead of Roosevelt's confiscation. Millions of Americans were willing to risk felony charges to hold on to their gold, and only 22 percent of the gold coins in circulation were turned in to the government at the going rate of $20.67 per ounce.

Once the gold was in the government's hands, the price was raised to $35 per ounce, an act of massive dollar devaluation. Dollar holders were swindled out of billions of dollars in the process.

Governments throughout history have displayed this insatiable hunger for the people's wealth. While confiscation and torture are effective tools for feeding this craving, manipulation of the supply of money and credit have proven to be even more efficient. These methods are so little understood by their victims, the people, that they are less likely to provoke violent resistance. In any case, the State intends its appetite to be fed. Like those addicted to powerful drugs, even when the utter impoverishment of the people and the collapse of the State itself become inevitable, one dose of deadly inflation generally demands another.

An example will illustrate why the State's contrived increases in the supply of money and credit result in higher prices. The entire economy of the United States changes very little overnight. There are about the same number of cups of coffee sold on Wednesday morning as there were on Tuesday. The number of houses in America doesn't change notably overnight. There are the same number of teachers in classrooms, clerks in stores, and doctors seeing patients from one day to the next. The acres of crops under cultivation don't change significantly overnight, nor do the number of loaves of bread and rib eye steaks in the grocery store, or flat-screen TVs in homes and automobiles on the road. It is of these things that wealth consists: the productivity of the people and the amount of goods and services.

But suppose overnight some Washington wizard waved a magic wand doubling the number of dollars in the nation, the amount of money in your checking and savings accounts, all the paper money in your wallet, in your dresser drawer, in your kids' piggy banks—in other words, doubling your nominal wealth and that of everybody else in the land. If you had five dollars, now you have ten; if you had a hundred thousand dollars, now you have two hundred thousand.

No doubt you would feel a giddy rush of prosperity with your morning discovery that your cash and bank accounts had grown twofold. Operating under the illusion that your circumstances had magically improved, you might set off on a spending spree, binge on more debt, and maybe throw money at Wall Street. Certainly all that would have been among the intended consequences of the sorcery—the State presuming always that managing the lives and behavior of individual Americans, including their proclivities to spend or save, is its legitimate function.

But would you really be twice as rich? Would everybody in America be able to double the size of their homes, dine out at restaurants that are twice as expensive, own twice as many cars? Would your lifestyle and that of everybody else in the land improve dramatically?

Of course not. The amount of real wealth—goods and services available—remains little changed overnight despite the fact that the amount of money in circulation has doubled.

It reminds us of a story told here in Arizona about an elder of one of the area's Native American tribes years ago when a battle raged over the proposed federal Daylight Saving Time law. After listening to the details about resetting all the clocks twice a year, he remarked, "Only a white man would believe you could cut a foot off one end of a blanket and sew it on the other end and get a longer blanket."

So it is with inflating the money supply. As in an auction, prices are bid up as people find more money in their pockets. But the blanket doesn't get any longer. The real wealth, the goods and services, remain unchanged, and before long prices throughout the economy adjust to the increased money supply.

If these activities add no new wealth to the picture, what is the point? There are several. Inflation enriches the State at the expense of the people. It is a clandestine tax, allowing the political classes to dodge unpopular votes to raise taxes. Money manipulation also redistributes wealth.

In an inflationary regime, not everyone gets the new money at the same time as they do in our example of the overnight doubling of the money supply. Some people get the new money first; therefore, they have access to the increased purchasing media at lower prices, before the consequent price increases become widespread and commonly recognized. Economists call this the "Cantillon Effect," named after the eighteenth-century economist Richard Cantillon, who first noted that the earliest recipients of newly created money profit at the expense of those who get it later. Like the other effects of inflation that are barely concealed forms of plunder, the Cantillon Effect has been especially profitable for the Deep State's Wall Street cronies.

Historically, inflations have been straightforward affairs. The kings of old debased the coinage by reducing its gold or silver content. If, for example, 1,000 gold coins came through his counting house, to which the king added copper to make 1,100 coins, his highness was enriched to the extent of the

100 additional coins, while the people eventually suffered the reduced purchasing power of the new, debased, cheaper coins. His royal gain came at their common expense.

Not so long ago, our own government issued paper dollars that it promised the rest of the world would always be redeemable in gold at a fixed rate. But the government was acting like any felon who intentionally writes checks without sufficient funds to cash them. As long as the bad-check scheme lasted, it enabled the politicians to buy votes with made-up money, and the State could appear able to afford and conduct warfare in faraway places like Vietnam.

When the US was found not to have the promised gold behind all the dollars it issued, it just openly repudiated its promise to redeem in gold. The holders of dollars were fleeced, paying the price in the reduced purchasing power of their paper money.

Europeans and others around the world who had accumulated dollars over the years in the belief that that the dollar was "as good as gold" not only suffered enormous losses, they had it rubbed in their faces when President Nixon's treasury secretary John Connolly later told them that "the dollar is our currency, but it's your problem."

Today, the dollar is your problem. Today, there is no pretense of the dollar being redeemable in gold or anything else. And none of the coins in circulation today consist of precious metals. While the Fed's activities today are more involved, the end result is often still referred to as "money printing" (a term for the artificial creation of money and credit that will be used throughout this book, both as a convenience and to treat the practice with the opprobrium it deserves). Still, for all the sophistication of today's Money Manipulators and the digital tools at their disposal, the simple, unrestrained printing of paper dollars always remains a monetary policy option.

Not long ago, then-chairman of the Federal Reserve Ben Bernanke, citing Nobel prize-winning economist Milton Friedman, said that if the need arose in managing economic conditions, the Fed could simply drop cash from helicopters into the waiting hands of people below. According to the theory, the Fed would generate consumer spending in this way, bypassing financial institutions like banks and employers altogether.

It is an idea of Keynesian absurdity. Why would merchants willingly sell their goods, or businesses willingly sell their production, for paper that rains down from the sky above without regard for the value of that paper tomorrow?

What assures savings and capital formation when it rains money? What provides money with exchange value when it covers the ground like the morning dew? What assures productive effort—work—when money falls like manna from heaven?

It is frightening to think that schemes such as helicopter money can be taken seriously, but improbable schemes are the coin of the realm in Washington circles.

Foreign Affairs is the journal of the Council of Foreign Relations, the organization that seems to drive much of the consensus policy of the country, and from whose membership the top officials of both Republican and Democrat administrations are regularly drawn.

In its September/October 2014 issue, *Foreign Affairs* wandered away from the calamity of its interventionist foreign policy consensus to offer equally calamitous interventionist monetary advice. The article offered its own helicopter money plan, without the helicopters. It advised the Federal Reserve to give the money it prints directly to the people. To make sure there is no mistake about this, the article, "Print Less but Transfer More," is subtitled "Why Central Banks Should Give Money Directly to the People."

Along the way, the authors even suggest the Fed issue its own debt, just like the Treasury does, and use the proceeds to speculate in the global stock markets.

The whole thing has the ring of adolescence. In fact, the authors even conclude with an eager sounding, "All it will take to change course is the courage, brains, and leadership to try something new."

Hey, kids! Let's try something new!

Quantitative Easing

This is the digital age and, at least for now, the Fed isn't simply printing money and shoveling it out helicopter doors. The Fed employs a more sophisticated sleight of hand. And it is all done electronically, without even the expense of old-fashioned paper and ink.

In the Deep State, the Federal Reserve expands money and credit by purchasing government bonds and other debt instruments, with money created out of thin air. With a few simple computer keystrokes, the Fed takes possession of these assets, buying them from banks or dealers, and "paying" for its purchases by making a book entry showing the bank has made a deposit in its account at the Fed.

With these monetary operations, the Fed has been directly responsible for each of the three gold bull markets in the postwar era, just as it has engineered more than a hundred years of calamities for the American people.

The Fed's unenviable track record consists of:

An endless sequence of booms and busts; the Great Depression and its prolongation; the stagflation decade of the 1970s; the wild whipsawing of interest rates that climbed to as high as 21 percent and were later forced to flirt with 0 percent, the latest policy that has created an unwholesome risk tolerance on the part of retirees looking for a return on their lifetime savings; the 1981–1982 recession, which was the worst downturn since the Great Depression, followed by another downturn even worse than the one before, the 2008 Great Recession; record waves of bank failures; millions of Americans losing their homes; the shifting of wealth from the poor and the middle class to the wealthy; and, the bailouts and therefore the perpetuation of badly managed banks.

Meanwhile, the Fed has been indifferent to the dual mandate given it by congress: maximum employment and price stability. Instead, the Fed has been targeting a 2 percent inflation rate as a policy objective. At that rate, a saver's $50,000 turns into about $30,000 in purchasing power in twenty-five years.

And in a quintessential act of the Deep State, during the mortgage meltdown of 2007 and 2008, while Americans were losing their jobs and homes, the Fed loaned more than $16 trillion at the expense of the American people and the risked solvency of the US, to foreign central banks and politically connected private banks and companies—even to foreign companies. It desperately tried to keep its financial chicanery concealed from the people.

But the single most destructive practice of the Federal Reserve, a power from which the Deep State derives its financial muscle, is the deliberate shrinking of the dollar's value. Since its inception, the Fed has destroyed 96 percent of the dollar's purchasing power. It does so because, like any inflator or currency counterfeiter, the Deep State derives much of its wealth and power from this practice. No wonder the Deep State doesn't want you to own gold.

But now, unchecked, unrestrained, and even unaudited for its history of malperformance, the Fed has taken its monetary madness to levels that would leave prior Fed officials clutching their hearts. Although the consequences are yet to be seen, during the last dozen years it has engaged in a monetary scheme so vast and reckless that it will leave America shaken to its core. And it has done so, as you will learn, in a time thick with heightened economic and geopolitical challenges for the dollar.

In the era of the mortgage meltdown, beginning in the fall of 2008 and continuing through 2014, the Fed began a new and aggressive program of bond buying. It was a program of staggering scale, comprised of three rounds of "quantitative easing," QE1, QE2, and QE3, the creation and spending of nearly $4 trillion.

So vast was this scheme—equal to more than 5 percent of the total world economy—that it simply had no precedent. The program was said to be structured to lower long-term interest rates in an effort to spur economic growth. But the Deep State Money Manipulators' objectives were many, all serving powerful constituencies. It is hardly debatable that its primary intent was to bail out the banking cartel that had created the Fed in the first place. And so, it purchased $1.7 trillion of non-performing and underwater mortgage-backed securities from the private banks and brokers. In buying these junk mortgage securities from the banks, it restored their balance sheets and created capital gains where otherwise there were losses.

That was not the only program at the time designed to bail out the banks. While the Fed put monetary policy in the service of its bank constituency, the $700 billion Bush bailout bill did the same thing with fiscal policy, providing billions to the banks with its TARP (Troubled Asset Relief Program) loans. Under this program the taxpayers bought the stock of troubled banks and loaned them money directly to the tune of hundreds of billions of dollars. It is a mistake to view such cronyism through a partisan lens, or to hope that the other party or the next election will deliver us from the Deep State' Money Manipulators. For while the bailout was created by the Bush administration, President Obama was pleased to share credit for it. Running for reelection in 2012, he boasted, "We got back every dime used to rescue the banks. We made that happen."

Yet that claim was only the usual Washington shell game.

To provide but one example of how the game was played, crony investment banker Goldman Sachs had taken a $10 billion TARP loan, which it bragged about paying back after only a few months, in June 2009. Few noticed that the firm was only able to pay back the loan because, just days earlier, it sold $11 billion of its troubled junk mortgage securities to the Fed, toxic assets that remained on the central bank's books.

Even as the Treasury was shoveling taxpayer money to the banks, the Fed became the 800-pound gorilla in the US Treasuries market. It purchased almost $2.5 trillion of federal debt instruments in its QE money-creating spree. In the absence of such a large buyer in the market, the Treasury would have had to offer higher interest rates to attract additional buyers of its bonds. This massive purchasing presence of the Fed in the bond market, with its specific objective of lowering interest rates, would please the elected classes since lower rates enable the State to borrow and spend more.

Support for federal borrowing and spending also pleases the military-industrial complex, about which President Dwight Eisenhower warned the nation. When Congress blew right past the cap set on defense spending passed in a fit of pretend fiscal responsibility in 2011, and piled an additional $80 billion on the warfare budget for 2018, champagne corks were popping in the arms industry. They should have been toasting the Fed, whose bond buying and interest rate manipulation made their windfalls possible.

But the biggest windfall of all was on Wall Street.

It was what Michael Hartnett, the chief investment strategist for Bank of America Merrill Lynch, called a "liquidity supernova." Since the Great Recession officially ended in June 2009, Fed actions drove US equity capitalization to more than $38 trillion. And it produced the lowest interest rates in five thousand years.

But isn't that inarguably a good thing? Perhaps for some, although not for everyone. For example, low interest rates are not good for capital formation, or for savers like retirees who rely on interest income. For behaving prudently with their money, these groups paid dearly for the Fed's interest rate distortions; skewing rates to benefit reckless financial institutions has cost savers as much as $600 billion. Low rates are not good when they mislead home builders about the real credit worthiness of home buyers, or when they convey misleading information about the underlying conditions of the economy, inducing business spending on capital goods that are ultimately unneeded.

It is not good when artificially contrived interest rates, or artificial prices of anything for that matter, favor one party's transactions at the expense of another; when they pit one class of people against another; when they communicate misleading information about real conditions of supply and demand; or when they create unsustainable bubbles in the economy.

These Fed activities are not good when they result in another collapse that destroys wealth and wreaks havoc on the economy, leaving Americans jobless and homeless as have prior Fed bubbles.

Amid the destruction and debris of the popping 2000 dot-com and the 2006 housing bubbles, Fed officials excused themselves by insisting that no one can recognize a bubble in advance. "I don't think we can know there is a bubble until after the fact," said Fed chairman Alan Greenspan in a Senate committee hearing in April 2000. His remarks came just weeks after the NASDAQ index peaked after having doubled over the prior year. And just before it collapsed in a steaming wreck that cost stock investors trillions of dollars.

However, sound money adherents, having learned from Mises, Hayek, Rothbard and others of the of the Austrian school of economic thought, know better. They would simply ask what drove the markets higher. Where did the money come from? Was it from new capital formation, from net new savings? In that case, you can have a sustainable market move. Or, was it driven by the artificial creation of money and credit by the central bank? That is the signature of a bubble.

The answer to that question is obvious in today's stock markets. With nothing more than computerized bookkeeping entries, the Fed created almost $4 trillion—equal at the time to about a quarter of the entire US gross domestic product (GDP)—*and bought assets with the newly created money!*

Christianity has the doctrine of the forgiveness of sins, but there is no equivalent in the economic realm. There is a cost for such monetary flimflammery. Every cost is borne by someone. Every debt will be paid. Or, as Milton Friedman famously said, "There ain't no such thing as a free lunch."

One person who did his best to redeem himself for his role in the affair is Andrew Huzsar. He was the Fed official in charge of its bond buying program. Five years after quantitative easing began, Huzsar wrote a *Wall Street Journal* column in which he said, "Despite the Fed's rhetoric, my program wasn't helping to make credit any more accessible for the average American. The banks were only issuing fewer and fewer loans. More insidiously, whatever credit they were extending wasn't getting much cheaper. QE may have been driving down the wholesale cost for banks to make loans, but Wall Street was pocketing most of the extra cash…

"Because QE was relentlessly pumping money into the financial markets…."

It was, he said, "the greatest backdoor Wall Street bailout of all time."

"I'm sorry, America," said Huzsar.

Did He Sell Out? Or Buy In?

Andrew Huzsar isn't the only former Fed official who has had second thoughts. Alan Greenspan, who served five terms as Federal Reserve chairman (1987–2006), has had first, second, and third thoughts that bring our discussion back to gold.

In a 1966 article, "Gold and Economic Freedom," before he became a State economist, Greenspan displayed an understanding of some of the reasons that States are at war with gold. He wrote:

An almost hysterical antagonism toward the gold standard is one issue which unites statists of all persuasions....

In the absence of the gold standard, there is no way to protect savings from confiscation through inflation. There is no safe store of value. If there were, the government would have to make its holding illegal, as was done in the case of gold. If everyone decided, for example, to convert all his bank deposits to silver or copper or any other good, and thereafter declined to accept checks as payment for goods, bank deposits would lose their purchasing power and government-created bank credit would be worthless as a claim on goods. The financial policy of the welfare state requires that there be no way for the owners of wealth to protect themselves.

This is the shabby secret of the welfare statists' tirades against gold. Deficit spending is simply a scheme for the confiscation of wealth. Gold stands in the way of this insidious process. It stands as a protector of property rights. If one grasps this, one has no difficulty in understanding the statists' antagonism toward the gold standard.

As Fed chairman, however, Greenspan abandoned his sound money ideals. His tenure reminded some of the remark by conservative columnist M. Stanton Evans that "when our friends get elected, they aren't our friends anymore." Instead of a concern for savings and value, under Greenspan's leadership the Fed's monetary policies and interest rate interventions blew two major bubbles: the dot-com bubble and the housing bubble. Both, inevitably, resulted in enormously costly collapses.

Greenspan expressed the view that the Fed had no expertise in stopping bubbles, but that it was better suited to try to clean up the mess after the bubble had burst. But he didn't do so well at cleaning up the mess either. The dot-com bubble, the first of three stock market bubbles in less than twenty years, burst in 2000. It had been driven by Greenspan's interest rate regime of the 1990s, which pushed rates down as a means of providing cheap liquidity to the banks.

When the dot-com bubble burst, Greenspan's cleanup efforts consisted of little more than interest rate manipulation once again, driving interest rates to lows that hadn't been seen in more than a generation. Between January 2001 and May 2003, Greenspan's Fed cut rates thirteen consecutive times. In this way the cleanup man created the next asset bubble, the housing bubble. When that bubble burst in 2007, it took the stock market down with it. Greenspan's successors, Ben Bernanke and Janet Yellen, thought to clean up the newest mess by driving interest rates down to levels never before seen. Hence, the recent asset bubble most apparent in the stock market.

Each of the three distinct stock market bubbles can be seen in the following chart of the broad-based Wilshire 5000 stock index. The first wave of Fed liquidity drove the dot-com bubble to its peak in 2000. The next wave, the housing bubble, took stocks to new highs in 2007. The crashes that ensued were extremely painful economic events for the American people. Yet the third wave, the most recent Wall Street bubble, is the steepest of the three and makes both the dot-com and the housing bubbles look modest by comparison. It peaked in January 2020, followed by the COVID-19 pandemic sell-off, and then another gusher of Fed liquidity that bounced the market back up.

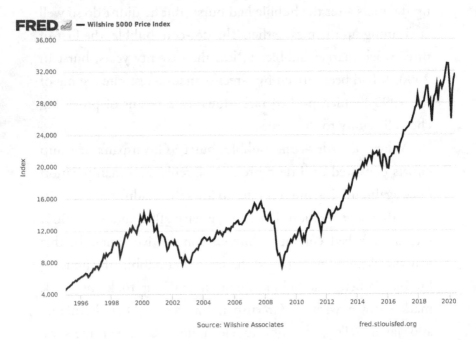

Source: Wilshire Associates   fred.stlouisfed.org

Whether Greenspan learned from these calamities or is simply bereft of further ambition at this stage of his life, is not apparent. Since leaving office, however, he has issued his third thoughts, understated warnings characteristic of his views before becoming a financial functionary of the Deep State.

In a 2015 conversation, Greenspan told market commentator Brien Lundin that the Fed is facing a serious problem. Lundin reported their conversation: "Specifically he said that the era of quantitative easing and zero-interest rate policies by the Fed...we really cannot exit this without some significant market event.... By that I interpret it being either a stock market crash or a prolonged recession, which would then engender another round of monetary reflation by the Fed.

"He thinks something big is going to happen that we can't get out of this era of money printing without some repercussions—and pretty severe ones—that gold will benefit from."

In a 2017 interview Greenspan warned, "The risk of inflation is beginning to rise.... Significant increases in inflation will ultimately increase the price of gold."

"We would never have reached this position of extreme indebtedness were we on the gold standard, because the gold standard is a way of ensuring that fiscal policy never gets out of line," said the former Fed chairman and bubble impresario.

What Has the Fed Done with QE?

"Pretty severe repercussions." "The greatest backdoor Wall Street bailout of all time." "A liquidity supernova."

It sounds serious, and so it is. It is so threatening that we want to specifically call your attention to the paragraphs that follow. Many of the other threats that will be discussed later in this book—trade and currency wars, the ending of the US empire, hot wars, the spread of banana republic economics across America—are very real. They are perilous fuel for a monetary crisis bonfire. Perhaps wiser heads can prevail, and their impact can be mitigated. Perhaps a trade war can be averted, or the empire can be allowed to end without desperate attempts to prolong it.

Perhaps.

But the rest of the quantitative easing story that we are about to tell is something few understand and almost no one talks about. It is the story of what the Fed has done with QE that cannot be undone. And now, after trying and failing to undo it, it has embarked on a new round of QE, faster even than the one before.

With its unprecedented 2008 to 2014 purchase of nearly $4 trillion in US Treasury, mortgage-backed, and other debt securities from the banks, the Fed took possession of those financial assets. It "paid" each bank by making an entry on its books showing that the bank had a deposit reserve in like amount on account with the Fed. The chart that follows shows changes in Federal Reserve assets beginning in 2008. Think of it as a log of anything the Fed has paid money for. Because the Fed can buy assets in the afternoon with money that didn't exist in the morning, it reflects the Fed's massive money printing during QE. We will refer to it again to see the impact of those activities on both interest rates and stocks.

You can see an attempt to roll back some of this reckless asset explosion in 2018. But by 2019 the Fed gave up and launched a new round of QE. With the frenzy of COVID-19 pandemic spending in early 2020, the Fed was at it again, buying securities, corporate debt instruments, and even junk bonds. On the far right the chart shows Fed assets moving straight up as the Fed quickly created $3 trillion.

What had taken the Fed five years in the Great Recession, it has now done in a matter of weeks.

Money printing has gone parabolic.

Source: Board of Governors of the Federal Reserve System (US)   fred.stlouisfed.org

QE was designed in 2008 to restore the balance sheets of the banks; what would have been bank losses were turned into gains. For the banks, it was a policy of socialized losses while profits remained private. Their toxic bonds and troubled assets were dumped onto the books of the Fed.

The operation was a godsend for Wall Street, bailing out its troubled mortgage-backed securities portfolios and driving interest rates down. The following chart shows the impact of

QE on interest rates. It is Fed assets again (solid line), along with the ten-year Treasury yield (in dashes) as rates were driven to historic lows.

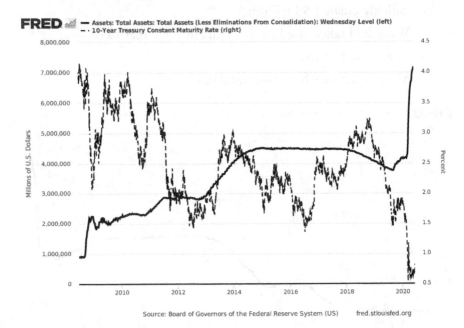

Source: Board of Governors of the Federal Reserve System (US)   fred.stlouisfed.org

Suppressed interest rates have forced people searching for a meaningful return on their savings to move further and further out on the risk curve and into the stock market. This is particularly unwise for older and retired people who need to minimize risk to their savings. Traditionally, bonds are preferred in their circumstance to insure a dependable, fixed return and to avoid the loss of principal in a stock market correction or crash. The portfolio squeeze these people are subjected to by the Fed's market distortions are likely to produce severe consequences in the years to come, especially among members of the outsized baby-boom generation.

The Fed's interest rate suppression supercharged the stock market. The next chart adds the Dow Jones Industrial Average stock index (the dashed line) to the Fed assets chart to make clear that it is the Fed's money printing and interest rate manipulation that lifted the stock market to record heights.

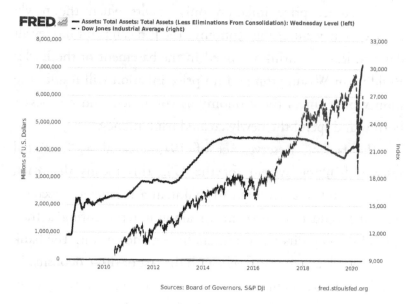

As the pandemic's effects began to ripple around the world in 2020 and stock prices fell, the Fed jumped with a splurge of money printing to save Wall Street and drive stocks back up as you can see on the far right of the chart. Was it a policy without risk? Could the Fed print money in response to any crisis without igniting consumer price inflation and without consequence for the dollar? For the answer we must look at what happened with the first rounds of QE from 2008 to 2014.

On its own, close to $4 trillion conjured out of nothing but an electronic bookkeeping entry by the Fed in QE represented a huge monetary expansion. It was equivalent to half of the M2 money supply (cash, checking and savings accounts, money market funds, etc.), about $8 trillion at the time. It was about a quarter of US GDP, an act of money creation so enormous that it might have produced a nightmarish inflation.

But it didn't. Instead, the newly created money was contained.

Consumer price inflation only results when the newly created money enters the economy. The Fed can print money all day and leave it shrink-wrapped in the basement of the Eccles Building in Washington and no price inflation will result. The money only enters the economy as consumers and businesses borrow and spend the newly created bank money.

The Federal Reserve Act of 1913 created a "fractional reserve" banking system for the US. This means that each member bank was required to maintain a balance on account with the Federal Reserve in an amount representing a fraction of the deposits its customers have made with it. The bank could issue loans to borrowers with the rest of those deposits. In other words, banks made loans in amounts many times greater than the amount of their required reserves. For example, if the reserve ratio is 1:10, a bank with $100 million in reserves with the Fed would be empowered to loan out ten times that amount: $1 billion.

A simplified model of fractional reserve banking's "money multiplier effect" illustrates how a deposit of, for example, $1,000 with Bank A would allow it, after setting aside a 10 percent reserve, to lend $900. That borrower then deposits the $900 with its bank, Bank B, which after setting aside a 10 percent reserve would be able to lend out $810. In turn, that new borrower deposits $810 with its bank, Bank C, which sets aside a reserve before making another loan to a new borrower, which is followed in turn by still another deposit.

This is high-power money and credit expansion, as one original deposit becomes the basis for subsequent rounds of additional bank credit. Changing the reserve ratio is a monetary policy that central banks have used to manage economic conditions, lowering the reserve requirement to loosen credit conditions at one time, raising reserve requirements to tighten them at another.

In addition to the reserves required to be maintained by the Fed, with the financial crisis of 2008 the Fed created what was an essentially a new category of reserves. "Excess reserves" were those beyond the amount the bank was required to maintain. The Fed pays the banks interest on these excess reserves.

For the most part, the banks haven't been lending against their new swollen reserves with the Fed. These excess reserves therefore represent money that does not otherwise enter the economy; it is not loaned out in the commercial banking system. It is money that is not used as capital for productive enterprises. It is money that does not grow the economy. It just sits on account at the Federal Reserve and earns the banks risk-free interest.

As long as these expanded reserves are not used as the basis for new loans, the money just sits on the Fed's books, humming along with negligible effect. Nevertheless, it is an unstable mass of monetary creation that is beginning to wobble. It can breach its containment unit whenever the banks choose to put that money to work in loans to their commercial customers. When that happens, it then becomes a massive increase in money and credit capable of causing a chain reaction of rapidly rising prices throughout the economy.

But don't take our word for it. Let us cite a 2015 research paper published by the Federal Reserve Bank of Minneapolis called, "Should We Worry About Excess Reserves?"

The author, an economics professor and Federal Reserve consultant, warns of sudden inflation because of bank action alone: "What potentially matters about high excess reserves is that they provide a means by which decisions made by *banks*—not those made by the monetary authority, the Federal Reserve System—could increase inflation-inducing liquidity dramatically and quickly."

The author then describes the highly leveraged monetary expansion that excess reserves, $2.4 trillion at the time he wrote, can produce:

> [E]ach dollar of excess reserves can be converted *by banks* into 10 dollars of deposits. That is, for every dollar in excess reserves, a bank can lend 10 dollars to businesses or households and still meet its required reserve ratio. And since a bank's loan simply increases the dollar amount in the borrower's account at that bank, these new loans are part of the economy's total stock of liquidity. Thus, if every dollar of excess reserves were converted into new loans at a ratio of 10 to one, the $2.4 trillion in excess reserves would become $24 trillion in new loans, and M2 liquidity would rise from $12 trillion to $36 trillion, a tripling of M2.

With the potential to triple the money supply, excess reserves are indeed worrisome. As you can see from the following chart, the amount of excess reserves quickly rose to over $2.5 trillion, and then consolidated around $2 trillion. Then, with the short-lived policy initiative "quantitative tightening" (QT), excess reserves fell to a range of about $1.5 trillion.

But suddenly in late 2019, the Fed embarked on a new round of quantitative easing. And excess reserves jumped again. Then, as the economic calamity of the COVID-19 lockdown struck, the Fed did something so remarkable that it could be described as bulldozing the entire foundation up which the central bank was erected. It simply eliminated the requirement described earlier that banks maintain a reserve balance with the Fed.

There is a reason the Fed was named the "Federal Reserve System." It was to be called *federal* to evoke the image of the US government. It was to be called a *system* to avoid the term bank. The operative word for its function is *reserve*. Instead of each bank depositing its reserves with another private bank as they had done, member banks of the new system were all required instead to deposit mandated reserves with the new central bank. This provision was used as a primary selling-point for the passage of the Federal Reserve Act in 1913: it would protect against regional panics and against bank runs. Its national might and the collective resources of its reserves would make the new system a bulwark against bank failures. Although it gave the banking cartel a monopoly on the creation of money and credit, the people would come to believe that it operated in the public interest. Eventually it became the central economic planner of American life.

Central bankers of earlier eras might have broken out in sweats had they lived to see it, but as the pandemic stay-at-home orders spread and businesses closed their doors in early 2020, the Fed announced that it "reduced reserve requirement ratios to zero percent effective on March 26, the beginning of the next reserve maintenance period. This action eliminates reserve requirements for thousands of depository institutions and will help to support lending to households and businesses."

With that the Fed's reserve function slipped down the memory hole. Just as paper money's function as a claim check for gold was forgotten and only the paper remained, now the Fed's primary function disappeared almost unnoticed. Only money printing and credit creation remain. And what is the need to maintain actual money reserves if the Fed can just print whatever it likes to paper over any bank problems?

Meanwhile, all the required reserves banks had on deposit with the Fed were set free. They became excess reserves overnight. As you can see on the right of the chart below, excess reserves shot straight up to $3.2 trillion.

Quantitative easing is only a continuation of what the Federal Reserve has always done. The monetary expansion seen on the charts above can be leveraged many times over by commercial banks, but this time on a scale that is unmatched even by the Fed's own standards. It is no longer possible to assume that the Fed's QE money creation will continue to sit inertly on its books forever, as evidenced by the chart showing that excess reserves came off their highs for several years. Like the breach of the reactor core of the Fukushima nuclear facility, it appears the Fed's money printing had begun to breach its containment unit; the money it created had begun leaking out.

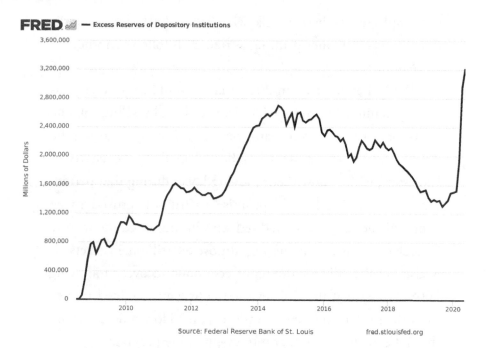

FRED — Excess Reserves of Depository Institutions

Source: Federal Reserve Bank of St. Louis   fred.stlouisfed.org

Excess reserves are one outcome of the Fed's QE machinations. Their presence is a living rebuke to the monetary authorities who naively believed they could knock out trillions of made-up dollars, buy assets with them, and not have any unwanted consequences.

The bubble the Fed has blown in the stock market this time is much larger than the dot-com or the housing bubble; the Fed's newest liquidity policies are more unstable than even those of the 2008 bust. And now excess bank reserves threaten radioactive levels of price inflation.

And runaway gold prices.

Despite a long track record of failure, confusion, and reckless monetary schemes that have destroyed the "good as gold" dollar and cost the people dearly, the Fed cannot stop. With trillions of dollars in money printing under its belt, and more contemplated, we have to ask what stops the Fed from additional sprees of money printing as one crisis follows another?

Nothing.

The Fed announced in 2017 that it would begin quantitative tightening, "shrinking" its balance sheet by selling off the assets, or not rolling over maturing bonds it bought during the 2008 to 2014 period. This is reflected in the prior charts of Fed assets, which show them moving lower during that period. However, carrying its QT promise to fruition proved to be another issue. The Fed is credited with having saved the world's financial system by purchasing almost $4 trillion in assets. It is also given credit for the tepid economic recovery following 2008. So, what if the Fed reversed course and drained money from the system and new recession set in? How quickly would the Fed embark on another money-pumping program?

It didn't take long to find out. When Fed chairman Jerome Powell spearheaded a modest Fed effort to normalize interest rates in December 2018, it prompted a tongue-lashing from the White House and Wall Street and a collapse of stocks, as the Dow Industrials quickly gave up more than four thousand points. It spelled the worst year for stocks in a decade.

Powell quickly reversed course, called a halt to the money tightening, and in a few weeks the market had recovered. The episode made clear that in addition to its other mandates, the Fed has taken on the role of the guarantor of the stock market.

"The Fed has become a self-declared vassal of Wall Street," says former Reagan budget director David Stockman, "meaning that no change in the current destructive policy regime is thinkable because trillions in inflated assets depend on its perpetuation."

Now, the Fed is doubling down. Its efforts to roll back the monetary expansion of QE before its ultimate effects are felt have failed. Its new money-printing regime is bigger and faster than the original quantitative easing. In the fourth quarter of 2019, well before the COVID-19 pandemic, Fed money pumping had already reached a breathtaking $413 billion. The Fed grew its balance sheet by more than 10 percent in three months. By some accounts, the central bank was panicking, desperately trying to suppress an outbreak of higher interest rates.

The Fed was already roaring into the new Twenties decade when the pandemic struck. Then it shifted QE into overdrive. It is massive monetary debasement, as each new dollar it creates will eventually devalue dollars already in existence.

Including those you own.

But Wait! There's More!

In discussing the leading financial activities of the State, economists talk about both monetary policy and fiscal policy. These two subjects are so fundamental to our economic vitality that they are receiving the lion's share of our attention. This chapter on monetary policy addressed the functions of the Federal Reserve and described some of its manipulation of the quantity and quality of money. A deranged monetary policy by itself can leave immeasurable suffering and disaster in its wake. But monetary policy is just one of the seven reasons that this will be the last dollar gold rush ever, that is, the last rush out of dollars and into gold.

Fiscal policy is another. It is the focus of chapter 2—*Debt Binging*. Fiscal policy encompasses the spending, taxation, and debt of the government itself. It may be hard to imagine anything that can compete with the Fed's long-term dollar destruction and its digital money confidence games. But as you will discover about the government's debt addiction in the next chapter, Washington's fiscal folly runs a close race to a regrettable finish line.

CHAPTER 2

DEBT BINGING

It Only Matters in the Real World

"How did you go bankrupt?" Bill asked.
"Two ways," Mike said. "Gradually and then suddenly."

—Ernest Hemingway, *The Sun Also Rises*

The Art of the Deal?

In 2016, with US government debt at more than $19 trillion, a famous investor of the billionaire class asked what would happen if interest rates climbed two, three, or four points higher. In that case, he said, answering his own question, "We don't have a country."

The billionaire investor had only said what was obvious: the US is in a precarious financial position. If its debts can't be repaid, they won't be repaid. The consequences of a US default in any form would quite literally be world-shaking.

Nevertheless, the alarm at the remark in establishment circles was immediate. In suggesting that US debt is not risk-free and questioning the outlook for future US solvency, the billionaire, a novice political candidate named Donald Trump, had committed what in Washington is called a "gaffe."

A gaffe, Michael Kinsley has said, is when a politician inadvertently tells the truth.

While Trump was correct about the existential threat the national debt poses, the soon-to-be president went on to show a dismaying inattention to the nuts and bolts of his subject. Trump first suggested the US debt could be renegotiated. Trump said, "I would borrow, knowing that if the economy crashed, you could make a deal."

Was Trump saying that US creditors could be forced to accept haircuts—a settlement for something less than the full value they are owed? Was he confusing US Treasury debt with non-performing real estate mortgages, defaulted construction loans, or the unpayable junk bonds with which he was more familiar?

If so, Trump wouldn't be the first politician with a dilettante's understanding of US sovereign debt. It has taken a succession of politicians of both parties, simply confused or indifferent to the certainly that debt must be paid back, to create the compounding debt crisis in which the United States government finds itself today.

The first time Hillary Clinton ran for president, she suggested issuing something called "baby bonds." This scheme would have required giving every newborn child a $5,000 account that would grow with interest until they could be redeemed in adulthood. Proponents, like Ray Boshara, the vice president of the New America Foundation, called for the yield on the baby bonds to be set to provide a $20,000 windfall at maturity. To provide the baby bond owners that much when they reach the age of twenty requires bonds that pay about 7 percent, a rate that ten-year Treasuries haven't seen in a generation.

And who are the working and taxpaying adults who would be made to pay off those baby bonds as the recipients become working and taxpaying adults? Year after year, as the rolls of yesteryear's giveaways reach adulthood, they themselves would be taxed to pay the redemptions for themselves and each subsequent year's maturing recipients.

Already American children are born debt slaves, responsible for the irresponsible spending of prior generations of politicians. In Hillary Clinton's village, the problem would have been compounded while a new bureaucracy would be created. Since nothing has the longevity of a government giveaway program, the now-grown babies would be paying the holders of new baby bonds *ad infinitum.* It is a burden that would add up to trillions of dollars of new debt to be serviced over the most productive years of the recipients' working lives.

Such harebrained, something-for-nothing, vote-buying schemes are dreamed up by economically illiterate politicians daily. They seem not to have confronted the problem of America's existing unfunded liabilities, including Social Security and Medicare. We will address that topic shortly, but proposals like baby bonds always sound suspiciously like cartoonish "gladly pay Tuesday for a hamburger today" promises. They are the economic equivalent of a perpetual motion machine

The same kind of confusion was implied in Trump's "let's make a deal" remarks on US government debt. Was he suggesting that he would have the government take on new debt, paying higher rates to pay off old debt instruments that carry lower interest rates? The responses to this free-lunch economics came quickly, and not simply from Trump's partisan and ideological opponents. Trump may style himself the "King of Debt," but his remarks screamed for reactions from those who understand the debt markets better than he.

One former Treasury official called the remarks "lots of very loose talk on a subject where there shouldn't be loose talk." A *CNNMoney* editor said the reaction on Wall Street and in Washington was that "Trump can't be serious." The *New York Times* account commented drily, "Such remarks by a major presidential candidate have no modern precedent."

Hounded by the criticism (one headline read, "No One Knows What the Hell Trump Is Talking About When It Comes to the Deficit"), Trump tried to call off the dogs. He explained to the *Wall Street Journal* that US government bonds are "absolutely sacred." But in continuing to insist that he would buy the debt back in the market at a discount, Trump was in a feedback loop of doom for US debt. If (and when!) investors perceive any kind of problem with the repayment of debt and the threat of its being "renegotiated" or restructured, then interest rates on US bonds will skyrocket to offset that risk. And if interest rates skyrocket, then, as Trump originally suggested, the compounding threat of insolvency feeds on itself.

In any case, the government's bonds will only be available on the market at a discount if interest rates go higher. Price is the inverse of yield. Stated differently, bonds and interest rates are like a teeter-totter: when interest rates move up, the prices of bonds go down. Think of older bonds yielding less than the new issues with higher returns. Because owning those lower-yielding bonds becomes less desirable compared to the higher returns available on the new issues, the market price of those older bonds will fall. But to redeem them, the government would have to issue new bonds at higher interest rates.

Conversely, if rates should move meaningfully lower than today's range of already historic low yields, the higher-yield bonds would cost more. They would be priced at a premium; their owners would not willingly part with them at a discount. If they were forced to exchange them for lower yields by some new legal mechanism, it would again shatter confidence in future US debt instruments. It is these considerations that no doubt caused the *Wall Street Journal*'s writers to ask Trump politely, "And so the US government should spend its money to go buy back its bonds?" It should issue bonds at higher interest rates to buy back bonds with lower rates? Or it should effectively commandeer bonds with higher yields, and force their holders to accept lower ones?

Finally, Trump offered up the one overarching truth of the matter. The future president said, "You never have to default because you print the money, I hate to tell you, OK?"

It was with that change of subject, pulling back the curtain to reveal the ultimate endgame of US debt and the dollar— we just print the money anyway—that the whole brouhaha went away.

Trump had uttered the truth about the Deep State's most powerful resource. Another gaffe.

Two years later, as president this time, Trump uttered another truth, one that explains why politicians have created the coming debt tsunami. Although candidate Trump had promised to pay off the national debt in eight years, it continued ballooning, growing by an average of more than a trillion dollars a year during his first three years. When aides tried to show him charts of the coming "hockey stick" debt spike, he replied with an insouciant shrug, "Yeah, but I won't be here."

It was better said in France by Louis XV's mistress, Madame de Pompadour, more than 250 years ago. "Après nous, le deluge."

"After us, the flood."

There's Plenty of It Going Around

Trump is not being singled out here for either his confusion or indifference about debt issues. Economic ignorance is common among fiscal policy makers of both parties as the following incident from the 2012 election illustrates.

Campaigning for reelection, Barack Obama showed up on the *Late Show with David Letterman.* Expecting an easy answer from a candidate he appeared to favor, Letterman asked the president, "Just how big is the national debt?"

Obama appeared visibly out of sorts for just an instant as he admitted that he didn't know "precisely."

Trying to be helpful, Letterman asked, "Is it ten trillion?"

That is when viewers learned that not only did the president not know "precisely" what the national debt was, he did not even know roughly.

It is one thing if the president doesn't know all the budget details about each of Washington's numberless bureaucracies. No one would reasonably expect him to know how much the Federal Trade Commission spends each year, or the specific budget of the Department of Housing and Urban Development. But the national debt is one of the two or three most revealing metrics of US solvency. It is one of the numbers that informed people watch. A clock on the streets of Manhattan has been displaying the climbing debt for passersby since 1989, when it was "only" $3 trillion. It is unthinkable that a president should opine about issues like his annual federal budget proposal or raising the national debt ceiling if he doesn't even have a handle on the gross national debt.

Since he didn't know the answer to Letterman's question, Obama employed the artful dodge. "The thing you have to remember about the national debt," he explained, "is that we owe it to ourselves."

No doubt that was part of the standard indoctrination of would-be community organizers and some-day Deep State functionaries enrolled at Ivy League institutions like Columbia and Harvard Law School. Intended to neutralize objections to increased State spending, "we owe it to ourselves" was a talking point of the statist left for a very long time. It has been collectivist poppycock from the beginning, since the logical conclusion is that if you owe it to yourself, why not just declare the debt settled? But it all turns on who "we" are. The federal debt is owed to specific bondholders, including individuals and funds with treasury instruments in their retirement programs. It is owed to businesses with payrolls to meet and retirees who depend on the bond payments to meet their living expenses. It is owed to parents saving for their children's education, to churches with bonds in their building funds, and to many others.

Just for the record, the national debt was $10 trillion when Obama was elected the first time. At the time of his appearance on Letterman's show, the debt had mushroomed to $16 trillion. It had grown by 60 percent in four short years.

But the talking points Obama learned in his school years make even less sense today since the US is increasingly dependent on the kindness of foreign creditors. More than a fourth of the national debt, $6.8 trillion, is owed to foreigners, including $2.3 trillion owed to just China and Japan.

In seeking to belittle the significance of the debt, Obama's claim that we owe it to ourselves ranks as one of the most foolish things said about the federal debt since Dick Cheney insisted that deficits don't matter.

The policy that the nation can spend its way to prosperity is the legacy of John Maynard Keynes, who gave big-spending, vote-buying politicians intellectual cover for their behavior. Keynesianism centers on the assertion that the government can "stimulate" the economy with deficit spending.

As the theory is practiced, the State runs deficits year in and year out, in good times and bad. Annual deficits that were only recently measured in hundreds of billions of dollars a year are now over a trillion dollars a year, without regard to the accumulation of debt.

As destructive as were Keynes's policy prescriptions, they are being supplanted today, at least among academics and politicians on the left, by something that will hasten the nation's confrontation with a cruel fiscal reckoning. The post-Keynesian Modern Monetary Theory (MMT) takes the idea that deficits don't matter because we owe them to ourselves, and blasts it into another galaxy. It lies behind the views of Bernie Sanders, Alexandria Ocasio-Cortez, and a growing cast of candidates and

officeholders who believe that the State can act like a cornu-
copia, a never-ending fount of eternal spending.

No longer must economics confront the reality that
resources are limited. The something-for-nothing fantasy of
MMT holds that while taxes may help the government manage
elements of the economy or tweak social behavior, they aren't
needed to fund the government. Nor is the issuance of bonds,
the State's means of borrowing, necessary. As long as the government is the monopoly issuer of currency (money that people
must use because it is the form in which taxes are demanded),
it can emit all the currency it needs to pay for the programs it
wishes, such as universal health care, guaranteed employment,
a guaranteed annual income, free college, the "Green New
Deal," and others. The government can print as much money
as it needs, and because it can do so, it need never default on
its debt. Leading MMT advocate and Stony Brook professor
Stephanie Kelton maintains that "anything that is technically
feasible is financially affordable." To which George Selgin of
the Cato Institute answers that there is a world of difference
between "technically feasible" and "affordable."

"For all I know," says Selgin, "we might populate the moon,
equip every US citizen with a Ferrari, or fill Lake Meade with
champagne, technically speaking. But I'm quite certain we can't
afford to."

In short, as the debt becomes an insurmountable obstacle
to the growth of the State, MMT offers to cut out the
middleman of borrowing. It proposes to supplant debt with
money printing on steroids, a cure worse than the disease. The
destructive illusion that wealth can be conjured out of nothing

has been cultivated by the fiat monetary practices of the Deep State Money Manipulators.

We now have the worst of both monetary policy and fiscal policy all at once: Modern Monetary Theory *and* helicopter money. Its presumptive adherents Bernie Sanders and Elizabeth Warren faded in the 2020 Democratic presidential race, but Modern Monetary Theory still won the day. On March 23, as Americans sheltered in place and practiced social distancing, the Fed announced that it would meet the pandemic crisis by buying anything and everything. It began spending trillions of dollars conjured out of nothing to fund the government directly and buy an endless supply of Treasury bonds, government-backed mortgage bonds, money market funds, and even corporate debt and junk bonds.

On the fiscal front, the very next day the president signed the $2 trillion CARES (Coronavirus Aid, Relief, and Economic Security) Act. ("I've never signed anything with a 'T' on it," quipped Trump as he approved the $2 trillion spending bill.) Like helicopter money, it delivered money directly to the people, payments of $1,200 for individuals ($2,400 for couples, and $500 more per child) for some 140 million Americans. Most of them were direct deposits so the helicopters never even had to leave the ground.

In a sidebar to our narrative, the CARES Act showed just how shameful things are in official Washington. The largest relief bill in history was presented to the American people in their distress, as their jobs and schools shut down, as they wondered in lockdown how they would pay the rent and feed their families, and as they watched the briefings promising deaths in the millions.

But the political classes don't like to let a good crisis go to waste, so they loaded the measure up with more pork than a processing plant. Former Reagan budget director David Stockman noted some of the line items as the CARES Act was being drafted to show how Congress had larded the emergency measure with pet projects and favors for its crony constituents, spending that had nothing whatsoever to do with the COVID-19 national crisis.

Here's just a small sample of what he shared:

- $25 million for additional salary and expenses for the House of Representatives
- $100 million to NASA
- $300 million to the National Endowment for the Arts
- $300 million for the National Endowment for the Humanities
- $30 billion for the Department of Education stabilization fund
- $300 million for Public Broadcasting
- $500 million to museums and libraries
- $7.5 million to the Smithsonian Institution for additional salaries
- $35 million to the JFK Center for the Performing Arts
- $315 million for State Department diplomatic programs
- $95 million for the US Agency for International Development

And so on.

With that kind of stewardship, it is no wonder that the US national debt is unpayable.

This Big!

Other than the fact that it is now $27 trillion and racing to $30 trillion, just how big is the US national debt? How can it be judged?

First of all, it is more than two times the revenue collected annually by all the governments of the world combined!

Another telling statistic is the total federal debt as a percentage of US gross domestic product. GDP is the most common measurement of a country's total productivity. (Since the calculation of GDP includes government spending, it is a sketchy number to begin with. Why, for example, if the government spends money for people to be unproductive, should that spending be counted as part of the nation's total productivity?)

In any case, the following chart reflects a spree of debt-financed government spending over the last generation. In 1980, federal debt amounted to 30 percent of GDP. Today, it is more than 100 percent of GDP. It climbed to about 100 percent of GDP in 2012 for the first time since the war spending of World War II, and it has stayed in that stratospheric realm ever since. In other words, the federal government's debt is more than all the productive activity of all the American people each year. The percentage of debt to GDP will move much higher as subsequent calculations of 2020 GDP show a steep drop, reflecting the COVID-19 economic shutdown, while trillions of dollars of related debt-financed spending are factored in.

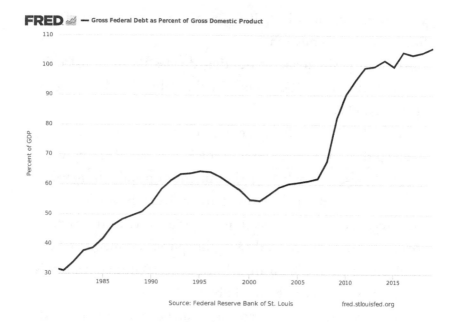

FRED — Gross Federal Debt as Percent of Gross Domestic Product

Source: Federal Reserve Bank of St. Louis   fred.stlouisfed.org

It might be helpful to think of this as though your credit card debt was more than 100 percent of your annual income, or that you owe more on your home mortgage than your home is worth.

Even that understates the problem, because your earnings or the equity in your home are your own. But America's GDP does not belong to the government and is not available to the government to address its debts; until it is taken from them by taxation, the productive output of America is the property of the people and companies that produce the wealth—each of which has debts of its own.

Another way to get a handle on the enormity of federal debt is to view it on a per capita basis. What is the pro rata share of the debt for each individual, and what has happened to it during the recovery that followed the Great Recession? In 2009, the debt was about $36,000 per person, or $144,000 for a family of four. In early 2020 it was $70,800 per person. That's $283,200 for a family of four.

Federal government accounting divides the national debt into two categories: "Debt Held by the Public," and "Intergovernmental Holdings."

Debt Held by the Public, more than $20 trillion of the total national debt, doesn't necessarily mean it is debt held by what we think of as the public or the American people. In general, it means the federal debt owed to individuals and corporations regardless of their location or nationality; to the Federal Reserve; and to state, local, and foreign governments. China owns about $1.1 trillion of US Treasury securities, which is classified as Debt Held by the Public.

The Treasury's other category, Intergovernmental Holdings, some $6.0 trillion of the total national debt, consists of securities held by US government trust funds, revolving funds, and special funds. The largest component of Intergovernmental Holdings is the Social Security Trust Fund, but there are others, including retirement funds for government employees and military personnel.

With the same intellectual fatuity of those who downplayed the significance of the debt by saying we owe it to ourselves, we now hear that the debt isn't actually more than 100 percent of GDP, since a quarter of the debt consists of Intergovernmental Holdings.

Those who argue this are saying that these debts are not real.

Why should $6.8 trillion owed to foreigners be treated as real debt and the trillions owed to the American people be thought of as a somehow less real debt?

You can decide for yourself if Intergovernmental Holdings should be considered real debts of the government. Imagine you are retired military. Your military service came with a promise of medical care and retirement earnings. Do you consider those real debts of the government? Or imagine you are a Social Security recipient. If you paid into Social Security all your working life and are now dependent on your monthly check to meet your living expenses, do you think that is a real debt? Or do you think that the monthly check or deposit into your account is something that you owe to yourself? If so, why not take the money out of your left pocket and put it in your right pocket?

Most certainly people receiving Social Security think intergovernmental holding debts are real, as do those paying into the program. Politicians didn't call military retirement a welfare program when people enlisted. Nor did they describe Social Security as a welfare program when it was enacted, as though the benefits people expect and rely upon are elective. In fact, the Social Security program is replete with terms like "insurance," "reserves," "funds," and even "trust." In effect, the people were told that they were too stupid or irresponsible to save for their own futures, so the government would do it for them.

Today the truth is no more complicated than this: the people who relied on those promises are the victims of an actuarial Ponzi scheme. The Deep State had better uses for the money that people paid in over a lifetime, and so it spent the money on secret wars and on programs to elect their political spear-carriers. It spent the money on foreign intrigue and crony windfalls. It spent the money and left behind an IOU.

The division of US debt into Debt Held by the Public and Intergovernmental Holdings is an attempt to delegitimize part of the debt. Is there any other institution in modern life that gets to decide which part of its debts it will honor and which it will not?

Unfunded Liabilities

Any discussion of Social Security introduces a larger topic of which it is but one part: the unfunded liabilities of the US government.

The unfunded liabilities are all the government programs and promises to pay that people depend on just as they depend on Social Security, but that, like Social Security, the government has made no or inadequate provisions to pay. They are future obligations that aren't funded.

Social Security is not even the largest of the unfunded liabilities. Medicare is much larger. Along with Medicaid and veterans' benefits, these are the leading unfunded liabilities of the US government.

We have already established that the Social Security Trust Fund doesn't exist except as an accounting fiction. The same goes for Medicare. On a cash flow basis, both are running deficits. Both spend more on current benefits than they collect.

By one reckoning, the State's unfunded liabilities exceed $144 trillion. (This does not even include the debt of state and local governments: they have about $3 trillion in explicit debt and another $5 trillion in unfunded liabilities of their own.)

Professor Laurence Kotlikoff of Boston University, using a method of calculation endorsed by seventeen Nobel laureates in economics and over 1,200 PhD economists for government accounting, calculated a couple of years ago that the "fiscal gap"—the difference between the federal government's projected financial obligations and the present value of all projected future tax, which is a measure of the unfunded liabilities—is $239 trillion—*almost nine times the visible or explicit debt!*

By either calculation, $144 trillion or $239 trillion, the amount is greater than the entire productive output of every human being in every country on the face of the earth. By any calculation, the bottom line is that these obligations cannot be paid. Taxes cannot be raised high enough to fund this mountain of political promises without taxable activity fleeing the country or grinding to a halt.

Who Eats the Debt?

Debt is always paid by someone. But that doesn't mean it is always paid by the borrower, as it should be. Often a borrower cannot pay his debts or refuses to do so. In the case of today's crony capitalism, the taxpayer is often made to pay debts owed to influential private companies. This is what happened in the bank bailouts when the mortgage securities in their portfolios went bad. The government made responsible people, those who had made sound decisions with their money, cover the losses of bankers who, supposedly sophisticated, should have known better than to make the reckless investments they made in toxic mortgage securities.

Often the taxpayers are asked to pay debts owed to arms merchants. This is implemented by the extension of credits, subsidies, or loan guarantees from taxpayers to foreign governments or warring factions who can't pay their bills. This extension of credit is risk free to the weapons makers. A real bonanza for the merchants of death occurs if they can arm both sides of a conflict.

During the Syrian civil war that began in 2011, the CIA armed and trained parties who fought with other factions armed and trained by the Pentagon. The profits involved provide ample incentive for the defense industry, as well as banks that make sketchy loans to warring states, to lobby for US foreign intervention in faraway places and in disputes in which the American people have no interest. This wealth transfer device of taxpayer guarantees is a favorite of the Deep State, one employed continually. An example of such a proposal is included in chapter 6—*Banana Republic Economics.*

The Debt Ceiling

A few words must be said to describe how dangerously unhinged members of the governing classes can be. When we are all threatened by the inevitable explosion of the debt time bomb and the collapse of the US capital markets, normal people understand that adding to the debt should become much more difficult.

Politicians are not normal people.

They are shameless in wanting less restraint on the growth of federal debt. Precisely because debates on raising the national debt ceiling—the statutory limit on government borrowing—are one of the few things the general public seems to understand, there is a movement afoot to end the exercise. President Obama's treasury secretary Tim Geithner urged that the statutory federal debt ceiling be eliminated entirely.

"The sooner the better," said Geithner. He was not alone. Roger Altman, a former senior Clinton administration official, called the need for statutory action to raise the debt ceiling "nonsensical" and an "anachronism." President Obama asked to be given the ability to raise the debt ceiling unilaterally. Then Senate minority leader, now majority leader, Mitch McConnell proposed the same thing

President Trump and current Senate minority leader Chuck Schumer have also agreed to discuss dispensing with the statutory debt ceiling entirely.

Don't be surprised if it happens. The debt ceiling was suspended for two years in August 2019. The *Daily Caller* reports that the 2020 Democratic presidential candidates conspicuously failed to mention the national debt on their web pages. The moderators of their debates also had little interest in the subject, while the "Promises Kept" section on President Donald Trump's reelection website made no mention of the national debt. Shining a spotlight on their fiscal irresponsibility, as debt ceiling debates do, is embarrassing to politicians of both parties.

They would rather work in the dark.

Having looked at the size of the debt and the pitiable prospect of its growth being restrained, the question is: how will the escalating debt be paid?

Or put differently, if it cannot be paid, how will the debt be resolved?

The government has several means of funding its current spending and servicing its debt: 1) it can impose taxes; 2) it can borrow the money; or, 3) It can inflate, or "print" the money. There are reasons that inflation becomes a preferred policy option of the State *in extremis*. A short comparison of each of the three means makes clear that a government's ability to pay its bills by taxation and borrowing are constrained. Because its ability to inflate is not similarly constrained (until the collapse of its monetary system), inflation becomes a preferred—and sometimes inevitable—choice of otherwise hopelessly indebted governments.

Taxation

A government's ability to raise money by taxation is constrained, first by the political cost. Raising taxes requires an affirmative political will and the displeasure of voters. This is unlike the government's exercise of its other options—borrowing or printing money—that often go unnoted by the public, at least at first. Taxation, on the other hand, is mostly overt. Politicians try to hide tax hikes, but it is hard not to notice when your take-home pay is reduced, or if you lose the deductibility of your home mortgage. It is easy to see who did it to you when you lose the deductibility of state and local taxes.

In addition to sometimes putting politicians in peril, the government's ability to raise money by taxation is constrained by diminishing returns. The government can raise *tax rates* all it wants, but raising *tax revenue* can be another matter. Writing about government debt in *US News & World Report*, economists James Harrigan and Anthony Davies explain:

> Whether higher rates generate more taxes depends on how people react to the new rates. Since the 1950s, the federal government's revenue has consistently averaged

about 18 percent of the economy. This has been true regardless of fluctuations in income, payroll, corporate, capital gains, and estate tax rates. There is much debate as to why this has been so; but there is no question that it has been so. Regardless of what tax rates it sets, the federal government seems only to collect 18 percent of the economy in taxes.

At some point, the peasants revolt against their tax-masters. In days gone by, a king who raised taxes risked a revolt. If today's State serfs don't rush out to buy pitchforks and storm the castle, they at least begin to alter their taxable behavior. There are many ways people and companies can modify their productive activities to avoid punitive taxation, ranging from producing less, to moving underground, to moving offshore. All three are in evidence.

US GDP growth has become much weaker with the growth of the State. In the 1950s and '60s, average real growth was more than 4 percent; in the 1970s and '80s, it was around 3 percent; for the ten years since quantitative easing was launched (2009 to 2018), GDP growth has averaged less than 2 percent.

The underground economy appears to be growing, which helps explain the shocking rise in the number of people who have left the work force. The offshoring of American jobs is well-known, as is the fact that US multinational corporations long kept as much as a trillion dollars of profits overseas rather than expose them to punitive US tax rates. This practice played prominently in the 2017 debate over the Trump tax bill. The point that raising tax rates and adding new tax measures does not necessarily produce more revenue is readily understandable if you consider that a 100 percent tax rate is one in which virtually all productive activity comes to a halt, thus producing no revenue.

Hiking taxes is the least palatable option for politicians, especially when their opponents are promising tax cuts. Unfortunately, unspoken in this contest of ideas is the simple economic truth that the level of taxation is equal to the level of government spending. Every dollar the government spends, it gets from someplace. Since both sides in these highly charged contests over tax rates, Republican and Democrat, conservative and liberal alike, generally support the growth of government spending, the contests between tax-hikers and tax-cutters are not debates about genuine tax reductions. They have, instead, to do with the visibility of the taxation.

Borrowing

While the level of taxation is equal to the level of government spending, government borrowing is less visible to the public, which generally fails to connect the dots to the deleterious consequences of mounting debt.

As is apparent in Washington's willingness to raise or suspend the debt limits, a government's borrowing ability may not be constrained by elected officials. But it can be limited by an unwillingness of creditors to loan it money. Where creditors see a poor credit risk, they generally demand interest rate premiums commensurate with their assessment of the risk. In some cases, they will be unwilling to make risky loans at any rate.

Even Washington establishment economists seem to agree that high debt is a drag on economic growth. Many academic researchers claim that this effect is especially observable when public debt rises to 90 percent of GDP.

Elevated levels of government debt create a vicious cycle visible in periods of reduced growth. Unemployment drives State social spending higher, even as tax revenue fails to keep pace. The gap between rising spending and falling revenue widens. Deficits grow and the debt mounts, further burdening the growth picture.

As the cycle continues, and because resources are finite, government borrowing for its nonproductive spending can crowd out productive private investment borrowing. Compare borrowing by government with borrowing by individuals. Suppose you decide to buy a new Mercedes-Maybach. Or a Lamborghini. In either case, you have expensive taste in cars. But before you drive it off the lot, you will want to look at the cost. What interest rate are you being charged? What will the payments be? How does that impact your ability to meet your other expenses? These are the considerations you and other consumers with finite resources make before buying a new trophy car or a used Toyota. Can you afford it?

Of course, experienced businessmen consider the costs of capital carefully as well.

The government is different in this regard. Some of its spending decisions may be discretionary. However, if tax revenue is insufficient to meet spending (including debt service), government borrowing decisions are not discretionary. They are existential. If the government needs money, it will pay any price. You may not be willing to buy a new car if the loan carries a double-digit interest rate, but in September 1981 the US paid more than 15 percent to sell ten-year bonds.

What choice did it have? Not to borrow the money? To default? To go out of business? The Deep State will do anything to hold on to power, and governments do not often willingly disband themselves. When creditors, foreign and domestic, become unwilling to lend to a debtor State for reasons of political and economic risk; when default or repudiation looms large; when the threat of sanctions, expropriation, the freezing of assets, and warfare are very real; creditors will find more hospitable places for their capital.

When the State borrows without the means to repay its creditors, inflation becomes inevitable.

Inflation

Consistent with the ideal that the American people were to be self-governing, both taxation and borrowing, at least so long as there is a statutory debt ceiling, require the approval of the people's elected representatives. However, the Federal Reserve System has betrayed this ideal, meaning the State has been able to engage in stealth taxation—inflation—to meet its fiscal needs.

Unlike borrowing, inflation is conducted independently by the Money Manipulators of the Deep State and is not directly dependent on the market cooperation of lenders. Unlike legislated taxation, inflation doesn't bear a direct and obvious cost for the elected classes.

Relatively speaking, inflation is a unilateral action of the State, so long as it is willing to make the inflated currency acceptable in the payment of taxes and enforce its use elsewhere in the payment system with legal tender laws. Mandating the acceptance of its debauched or faux currency is business as usual in States deeply dependent on inflation.

Unapproved by the public and conducted without legislative debate, inflation is determined in the dark by unelected and virtually unknown bureaucrats. These are mostly statist academics, who make decisions about money supply and credit conditions without either oversight or objective standards. As compared to the discipline of the gold standard, bond market observer James Grant says the US is now on "the PhD standard."

Considering the Fed buys government bonds, creating money and credit conditions by turning government debt into bank reserves, informed people may wonder why the Treasury Department doesn't just print the money to buy its own bonds. It would be no less a counterfeiting scheme, and it would vastly simplify the process.

The answer is that the Fed acts as a cutout for the Deep State, with its machinations hidden from public view and insulated from lawmakers in a way the Treasury's operation are not. Indeed, the Fed's byzantine practices are specifically designed to conceal its activities. It strenuously resists being audited to keep them concealed.

Eventually details leak out, and the Fed's cronyism and Deep State enabling can be glimpsed and compared to a more transparent public process. In September 2008, the American people watched the $700 billion Bush bank bailout bill work its way through Congress. They did not like what they saw. As the phones at the Capitol melted down with the revolt of the masses, members of the House voted the giveaway down, 208 to 225. It was a short-lived victory. Given some arm-twisting by the "DC leadership," and who knows what kind of backroom deals, two days later the bailout was voted on again. This time, it passed, 263 to 171.

Contrast that with the Fed's shrouded activities in the same episode. Operating clandestinely, it extended $16 trillion of loans and the credit of the American people, *an amount greater than the entire GDP of the country*, to crony companies and banks at home and abroad and even to foreign governments.

There was no outcry from the people because it was all done in secret.

Just as the Fed engages in secret cronyism, it similarly enables Deep State wars. Economist Murray Rothbard pointed out that the Federal Reserve Act took effect in November 1914, just in time for World War I. While the Fed was instrumental in funding the US war effort and providing massive loans to its allies, it "roughly doubled the money supply during the war, and prices doubled in consequence."

Inflating Debt Away

In deeply indebted nations, the authorities often turn to inflation as a means of managing the debt burden. An example is the Weimar Republic, Germany after World War I, which struggled under the crushing external debt of war reparations imposed by the victorious Allies. One can readily imagine a country with debt so high, say $27 trillion in explicit debt and hundreds of trillions in other liabilities, that there is no prospect that its bonds coming due now can be paid other than by continually rolling the debt forward by the issuance of new bonds tomorrow.

Never mind the culture- and commerce-destroying chaos visited on the people when the State tries to inflate away its debt. It is, nevertheless, a strategy that often appeals to State monetary and fiscal authorities. After all, a 6 percent inflation rate depreciates a $27 trillion debt by $1.62 trillion a year. Investor Warren Buffett meant his description of the inevitable adaption of such a debt-extinguishing strategy to refer to the US: "A country that continuously expands its debt as a percentage of GDP and raises much of the money abroad to finance that, at some point, it's going to inflate its way out of the burden of that debt."

Low rates of inflation can't evaporate the State's debt. They don't do the trick because maturing government bonds must be rolled over, or reissued, eventually at higher rates as the market adjusts to existing and expected future inflation. Rising inflation can decimate the productive economy, but a little inflation isn't enough to evaporate the debt. It takes a lot of inflation.

But just because something doesn't work doesn't mean it won't be tried. Monetary authorities who are willing to print $7 trillion or more to buy government bonds and the toxic assets of banks are quite capable of printing trillions more in pursuit of other specious objectives. State debtors have resorted to inflation extremes many times under the burden of otherwise unpayable debts. Consider just a few historical examples of debt-driven inflation.

After World War II, Hungary was ruled by the Soviets, who were quite willing to see the country reduced to economic rubble. Accordingly, at the end of the war, Hungary's inflation persisted to the point that in 1946 the government issued notes in the denomination of 100 quintillion of its currency, the pengo.

Rivaling Hungary's inflation is the more recent hyperinflation in Zimbabwe. It reached epic and memorable proportions in 2007 and 2008. Socialism and land grabs under the Mugabe government led to a collapse in productivity and, therefore, a collapse in tax revenues. As the deficits grew, inflation became the policy of choice. In the ten years from 1998 to 2008, Zimbabwe's annual inflation rate climbed from 32 percent to 11,200,000 percent. During that period, the finance minister, Gideon Gono, who became something of a celebrity for the absurdity of his policies, called on merchants to see if they had illegally raised prices. If they had, he personally had them arrested. By 2017, less than ten years after its storied inflation, Zimbabwe was back in the hyperinflation business once again.

The inflation in Weimar Germany a century ago is history's most famous. It deserves to be remembered because it took place in a modern and powerful industrial nation, and because the consequent destruction of the middle class in Germany prepared the soil for the flourishing of National Socialism, Adolf Hitler, and World War II.

The gold standard was abandoned in Germany in 1914 to enable the government to fund its war operations by borrowing in paper money. By 1919, prices had already doubled. Then, with the debt burden of war reparations, the money printing got underway in earnest. From the end of 1922 to December 1923, Germany's wholesale prices had risen over 85,000,000,000 percent.

The "sack of Germany" is how one account described the late stages of the inflation there: "Anyone who possessed dollars was a king in Germany. A few American dollars, still backed by gold, would allow a man to live like a millionaire. Foreigners swarmed into the country, buying up family treasures, estates, jewelry, and art works at unbelievably low prices."

If foreign currencies were prized, so much more so was gold. However, calculating the gold price in terms of the hyperinflating currency is only an academic exercise, one worthless in practical application because nobody much cared to exchange gold for German marks. The price of an ounce of gold, which had been 170 marks in 1919, reportedly soared to 87 trillion marks.

Of the many lessons to be learned from the German inflation, one noted by economic journalist Henry Hazlitt more than forty year ago, is timely today: "In the German hyperinflation of 1919–1923, it is true, the average price of stocks increased billions of times, but average wholesale prices increased many more billions of times. The net result was that, at the end of the inflation in December 1923, the average price of stocks was equivalent to only one-fourth their gold value in 1913."

The inflation rate in Nationalist China during the years 1947 to 1949 topped 5,000 percent. Merchants who defied the price controls, which are generally imposed in tandem with inflation, were dragged into the streets and shot. As a consequence, the government's support among the people deteriorated, much to the advantage of Mao Zedong and his Communist revolution.

The French Revolution from 1789 to 1799 is justly famous for its brutality and bloodshed. Merchants faced the death penalty for the crime of simply asking customers what form of currency they intended to use, the State's increasingly worthless paper or gold or silver. More than sixteen thousand persons met their death on the guillotine during the Reign of Terror. Annual inflation topped 1,100 percent.

Many are the South American inflations, including that in Peru in 1990 during which prices doubled every thirteen days. From 1986 to 1991, during the reign of Nicaragua's Sandinistas, inflation there was more or less continuous. The top rate was 14,000 percent. Endless budget deficits were behind Argentina's inflation of the 1980s. Inflation reached an annual rate of almost 5,000 percent in 1989. Venezuela, Bolivia, Brazil, Chile...inflation is often a way of life in South America. We will look more closely at banana republic economics in chapter 6.

One doesn't need hyperinflation to trigger a bull market in gold. The official US inflation rate hit 12.2 percent in 1974 during the first of the postwar bull markets. In 1979, during the second bull market, inflation reached 13.3 percent.

With the absurdity of prices doubling in a matter of days and hours, one must ask why governments do it. Like the first hit of an addictive drug, in the beginning the effects of inflation may seem beneficial. "In fact," says Murray Rothbard, "counterfeiting can create in its very victims the blissful illusion of unparalleled prosperity."

Federal Reserve officials have been targeting a completely arbitrary inflation rate of 2 percent as the goal of their monetary policies since the mid-'90s. It is a goal without any real economic justification and in fact produced both the dot-com and the housing bubbles. Even so, discussions are underway among Fed officials about raising that target.

But inflation is not a light switch that can be turned on and off, although that is precisely how the Fed attempted to manage money and credit conditions during the 1970s. It churned the Fed funds rate from 3.5 percent to 13 percent, then down to 4.75 before it pushed the rate back to 10 percent and on to 15.5 percent and finally, in 1980, to 20 percent. It changed rates more than twenty times in 1973 and 1978.

Once the genie of money printing has been let out of the bottle, its impact on prices and the timing of that impact are not foreseeable in detail. They are dependent on a vast market of millions of actors and their subjective decisions, and indeed, on those of dollar holders worldwide.

Once the genie has been let out of the bottle, it cannot easily be put back.

High Debt and Low Rates?

Washington's out-of-control spending and its wobbly tower of debt is the second dynamic behind the coming gold and silver bull market. Below is another instructive look at the correlation of the national debt and the rise in gold prices. The two have gone together like a hand in a glove for a very long time. The divergence since 2013, involving trillions of dollars of Fed interventions, suggests that gold had some catching up to do to reflect today's increased debt. And indeed, that resumption began in earnest in the summer of 2018. In less than eighteen months, from trough to peak, gold climbed 40 percent, a powerful bull market by any definition.

Like the Fed's money printing, federal debt has similarly grown to inconceivable proportions. It cannot be paid. To put its immensity into perspective, at $1,250 per ounce, the average gold price in 2016, it would take more than three times all the gold ever mined in the history of the world to pay off the US national debt.

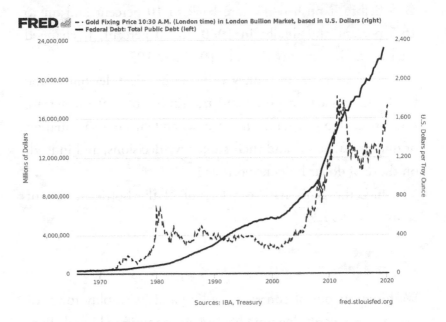

For the time being, we have historically high debt and the lowest interest rates in history. The two—record high debt and record low rates—cannot peacefully coexist. Together, the combustible mix of the debt and the Fed's monetary practices are all it takes to launch another spectacular bull market in precious metals.

But this time there is much more fuel ready to be ignited.

Part Two

COMING EVENTS

CHAPTER 3

TRADE AND CURRENCY WARS

Race You to the Bottom!

I do wish someone would tell me what would be the use of large
standing armies and powerful navies if trade were free.

—Frédéric Bastiat

Trump the Trade Warrior

It is a great irony of life that but for Rocket Man and his brandishing of nuclear arms, we might have been a year further along spiraling into a new global depression. Only an attempt to secure China's cooperation in reigning in the North Korean dictator kept President Trump from initiating a trade war with China in his first year.

Despite his repeated promise on the campaign trail to label China a "currency manipulator," on his first day in office (a prelude to the imposition of US tariffs), President Trump soon tweeted, "Why would I call China a currency manipulator when they are working with us on the North Korean problem?"

Soon after taking office, Trump was talking up his own currency manipulation, and talking down the dollar. And praising Fed interest rate policies that make the dollar worth less.

In joining the currency wars—the best that Trump could say about a strong dollar is that "it sounds good"—the president could have explained that as countries compete to depreciate their currencies, they raise the cost of living along the way, producing price inflation for their people. Since all the currencies can't be the cheapest, in the end they are all simply depreciating their currencies in tandem against the price of gold.

In his second year, fourteen months into his presidency, Trump announced tariffs of $50 billion on Chinese goods entering the US. Another 10 percent tax on $200 billion in additional goods soon followed.

Perhaps its only coincidental: Trump broke the ice with North Korea's Kim Jong-un at their June 2018 Singapore meeting; the first round of Trump's China tariffs went into effect a month later.

Before long, a joint study by the Federal Reserve Bank of New York, Princeton University, and Columbia University found that by the end of 2018, Trump tariffs were reducing US incomes $1.4 billion a month.

China's quick reciprocation provides a glimpse at the cost of trade wars and the ways they escalate. China imposed tariffs of up to 25 percent on American agricultural products.

The agricultural community was slammed. The USDA estimated that farm exports would fall by $1.9 billion in 2019.

Some 60 percent of American soybean output had been going to China. With the trade war, exports to China plummeted. Brazil stepped in to help China meet its soybean demand. That development threatens to have a long-lasting impact on US market share.

Farmers' losses were compounded as prices fell, since even what they were able to sell elsewhere was sold at lower prices. Their lost revenue soon ricocheted out to companies like tractor manufacturer Deere & Company, which had to cut earnings estimates for its farm equipment division.

By July 2018, the cost to farmers was so great the Trump rolled out a Depression-era program to provide up to $12 billion in welfare for farmers.

Early in 2019, after a year of tariff wars, Trump was asking China to remove all import tariffs on American agricultural products. Reporting on the president's request, an Associated Press story noted somewhat dryly that "Trump doesn't mention that the Chinese-imposed tariffs are in retaliation for the actions he took."

As the COVID-19 virus spread around the world, trade restrictions added needless burdens to the crisis. The maker of Purell, the hand sanitizer that quickly disappeared from store shelves, had to seek government relief on taxes to import its dispensers. Home Depot petitioned the government for tariff relief to meet the surge in demand for thermometers as the pandemic grew. General Motors, suddenly tasked with producing thirty thousand critical care ventilators for America's hospitals, ran into both needless expenses and slowdowns in acquiring the components for the health emergency. The ventilators consisted of seven hundred parts, said GM; among the components it identified in its request for tariff relief were gaskets, seals, and grommets. These are not items that bureaucrats would likely be equipped to identify as potentially critical health care items when they draft trade restrictions.

History teaches that devaluations, tariffs, and trade restrictions produce swarms of retaliations and powerful aftershocks that are seldom foreseen by politicians. Many other consequences, if not in their precise manifestations, are predictable in general. Most stark and inevitable is a trade war's overhanging impact on the very visible problem of the US debt detailed in the last chapter. It is very foolish to ignite hostilities with your major creditors. In recent years, foreigners have funded more than a fourth of the US government's debt; China is among the largest of those creditors.

So intent is Trump on waging aggressive and virulent trade and currency wars that it deserves its place as the third economic event that can fuel *The Last Gold Rush…Ever.*

Trump is only one among an endless secession of trade interventionist presidents. President Obama, doing the bidding of the United Steelworkers, imposed a 35 percent tariff on tires made in China. Early in his presidency, Bush imposed tariffs on steel imports that ranged up to 700 percent on some Chinese steel pipe.

Just as it is clear that powerful union bosses were behind Obama's tariffs, politics were behind the Bush tariffs as well— and not very good politics in either case. Obama's tire tariffs cost US consumers over $1.1 billion in higher prices on both Chinese- and US-made tires. At the same time, US chicken producers lost $1 billion in sales to China due to that country's trade retaliation. The higher costs of imported steel under the

Bush tariffs resulted in shortages for American manufacturers of steel products who soon found their goods at a price disadvantage compared to their foreign competitors. Higher steel prices cost two hundred thousand Americans their jobs and $4 billion in lost wages.

If Bush was hoping to win votes among labor union members, the European Union quickly figured out how to count future votes as well. It threatened to retaliate against Bush's steel tariffs by imposing tariffs on American automobiles and oranges, a strategy designed to make Bush pay an electoral price in toss-up states Michigan and Florida.

In less than two years Bush capitulated, and the world was pulled back from another trade war.

While other presidents have tiptoed onto the trade battlefield in the service of certain manufacturers and unions, Trump is another matter. He is personally devoted to warring over trade, or at least risking a trade war to test his skills in the art of the deal.

In addition to a trade war with China that was among the centerpieces of his campaign, other countries were in his crosshairs. And like Bush before him, Trump slapped big tariffs on Canadian lumber. That didn't help American home builders or home buyers. Along the way, Trump signed a Russia sanctions bill so draconian that Russia's prime minister said it amounted to a "full-scale trade war."

When Trump signed the Russia sanctions bill in August 2017, it triggered a predictable reaction. At the time, Russia was a meaningful creditor of the US, holding more than $100 billion in US Treasury securities. A year later, in 2018, it had reduced its holdings to $14 billion, and eventually to $8.5

billion two years after the bill was signed. Over the period, Russia beefed up its gold position, adding five hundred tons to its central bank reserves.

The rest of the world recognized Trump as an inveterate trade warrior from the beginning and sensed that world commerce was on verge of something big. Here is a sample of news story headlines from the president's first year in office:

- EU Threatens to Retaliate Against US Sanctions on Russia
- China Threatens with Trade War Retaliation
- Is Trump trying to start a trade war with Canada?
- Trump's signal of protectionism raises risks of trade wars, retaliatory tariffs
- Trump's new antitrade push may force retaliation from 2 key allies—and hurt US homebuilders
- Trump's trade war: Threats against Mexico could affect consumers
- Germany worried Trump may start trade war with Europe

Wringing cooperation on North Korea out of China proved not to be enough to long defer Trump's hunger for a trade war. Reports describe the president, with senior staff assembled in the Oval Office, rejecting negotiated settlements of trade disputes with China; he was short and to the point: "Tariffs. I want tariffs."

Economist Don Boudreaux frequently writes open letters to expose economic misconceptions voiced in the public debate. In a November 2017 letter to the *Wall Street Journal*,

Boudreaux took on trade interventionist comments by Trump administration official Wilbur Ross:

Editor:

Commerce Secretary Wilbur Ross boasts that the Trump administration will escalate what you describe as its "fight against 'dumped' goods" ("The Coming Aluminum War," Dec. 4). Well. Forget that the bureaucratic process for determining if imports are "dumped" in America is notoriously biased in favor of a finding of "dumping." Instead note two features of this Trumpian battle.

First, because imported goods are inanimate and come to America only because Americans choose to buy them, the administration's fight is not against the goods but, rather, against the flesh-and-blood Americans who voluntarily purchase the goods. As is true of all trade restrictions, this one at root is a restriction on the freedom of domestic citizens to maximize the values of their incomes.

Second, this Trumpian fight against "dumping" reveals the ignorance and inconsistency of Ross and others in Trump's troupe of economic nationalists. If the Chinese really are selling aluminum to us Americans at excessively low prices, then the Chinese are voluntarily redistributing wealth from themselves to us. They're giving us gifts. Therefore, a lieutenant of someone who famously wants to "make America great again" and who worries that American wealth is draining into China and other foreign countries should applaud Chinese "dumping"; that person should agitate not to end dumping but to increase it. And yet Ross does just the opposite—a fact that implies that he is either hopelessly ignorant or dangerously disingenuous.

Sincerely,

Donald J. Boudreaux
Professor of Economics
George Mason University

The Last Great Trade War

There was not much to restrain Trump when he let loose the dogs of trade war. Trade restrictions are popular on both sides of the aisle; Senate minority leader Chuck Schumer has been a trade warrior for a long time. In their personal shopping and spending practices, the American people behave like supporters of free markets. Sensibly, they want to get the best products for the least money. But because they know the American economy is in relative decline, they are susceptible to economically specious appeals to their patriotism and other blandishments of trade interventionists.

That the economics of free exchange, as Ludwig von Mises noted, have been proven "beyond refutation," is not something we can expect the political classes or the people themselves to know. Says Mises, "The final result of restrictions placed on foreign trade is the general decline of the productivity of labor and, therefore, of standards of living. In this way, production ceases to occur in places where a high return may be achieved and moves to others where, with the same investment of capital and labor, much lower returns can be obtained. The classic doctrine of free exchange...has never been refuted. All objections to it turned out to be unfounded."

A grounding in economics is not to be found among the political classes that intervene blindly in economic issues as though it were their job description. As they blunder about, some familiarity with the last great trade war would be helpful in anticipating what to expect from the newest trade wars.

In May 1929, five months before the stock market crashed, the House of Representatives passed a version of the Smoot-Hawley Tariff Act. The most destructive trade war in history was beginning to take shape. Despite his subsequent reputation as a champion of free markets, it was clear from his record that president Herbert Hoover, who took office in March 1929, was an economic interventionist.

The stock market climbed throughout the Roaring Twenties on the Fed's inflationary policies, which in the eight years between July 1921 and July 1929 had jacked up the money supply by 55 percent. By the time the market crashed in October 1929, it was clear that Hoover tariffs would be the order of the day. Foreign governments could see what was coming. They began warning of retaliatory measures. If they couldn't sell goods in American markets, they would not be willing to buy America's exports.

Their warnings weren't enough to stop Hoover from signing Smoot-Hawley in June 1930. It is hard to find a serious economist who doesn't agree that Smoot-Hawley exacerbated the Great Depression, but in *The Way the World Works*, Jude Wanniski, who carefully traced the legislative progress of Smoot-Hawley and the market action that foreshadowed the coming crash, makes his case explicitly: "The stock market Crash of 1929 and the Great Depression ensued because of the passage of the Smoot-Hawley Tariff Act of 1930."

Smoot-Hawley dramatically raised already high taxes on goods coming into America. (Tariffs are a tax, in this case a tax on goods paid by the American people. Therefore, in the rest of this section we will generally use the word tax instead of tariff in the interest of clarity.) Smoot-Hawley applied to twenty thousand items imported into the US and raised the average tax on tariffed goods to almost 60 percent.

After Hoover signed the bill, American imports fell sharply, from $4.4 billion in 1929 to $1.5 billion in 1933. If foreigners couldn't sell goods to Americans, they had no dollars to buy American-made goods. It was a calamity for producers of American exports, which fell from $5.4 billion to $2.1 billion in the same period.

Italy, France, and Germany were among the scores of countries that responded by raising taxes on American products coming into their countries. They focused on products in which America led the world—automobiles and radios—raising taxes above 50 percent. Italy's retaliation was provoked by the high taxes Smoot-Hawley slapped on its olive oil exports, never mind that the US was a negligible producer of olive oil itself. Italians reacted with anger, which they directed at drivers of American cars. Eventually, Italy raised taxes on American autos to almost 100 percent. American dealerships in Italy closed and another share of American manufacturing took a hit. Even Canada, the US's largest trading partner, was provoked to enact retaliatory taxes, battering profitable US exports to Canada.

It was the same around the world. The taxes tanked Japan's trade with the US, which had been 15 percent of its exports, and widened the gulf between the two countries. In clobbering world commerce, the US hammered its own. Between 1929 and 1932, global GDP fell by 17 percent, but the drop in US productivity was steeper, off 26 percent.

As noted in the previous chapter, higher tax rates do not necessarily produce more revenue. Taxes collected from imports plummeted.

One side effect of the sliding economy was that foreigners and Americans alike lost faith in the dollar and began withdrawing their gold from US banks. They were wise to have done so, as it would not be long before Franklin D. Roosevelt declared war on gold. Fittingly, both Smoot and Hawley lost elections in 1932, as did Hoover himself, defeated by FDR, who ran on an anti-tariff platform, a position he characteristically abandoned.

Trade wars are not good for the stock market. The Dow Jones Industrial Average did not return to its 1929 high for a generation, until 1954.

Currency Wars

When the international monetary system was linked to gold, the latter managed the interdependence of the currency system, established an anchor for fixed exchange rates and stabilized inflation. When the gold standard broke down, these valuable functions were no longer performed and the world moved into a regime of permanent inflation. The present international monetary system neither manages the interdependence of currencies nor stabilizes prices. Instead of relying on the equilibrium produced by automaticity, the superpower has to resort to "bashing" its trading partners which it treats as enemies.

—Robert Mundell, Nobel Laureate in Economics

You know there is something surreal about the international monetary order when you witness countries berating their trading partners for selling them goods too cheaply.

Imagine the customers of your favorite neighborhood restaurant constantly yelling at and scolding the proprietor because his food isn't more expensive. It's as if the governments of the world want their citizens to get less for their money. To that end, they debase their currencies on the pretense that it will make the people wealthier.

Of course, most people judge their wealth by what their money will buy. Yet in the topsy-turvy world of central banking and fiat money, things are a little different.

The largest, most influential companies and crony capitalists persuade the governing classes that if the purchasing power of the currency is eroded, foreigners will buy more of their products: airplanes, automobiles, computer software, motion pictures, and so on. But in reality, it is a wealth transfer to those manufacturers from the rest of the people who must buy food, energy, and countless other imported goods that are in whole or in part made more costly thanks to currency value manipulations.

Such a wealth transfer by means of currency manipulation calls to mind the words of the French economist and statesman Frédéric Bastiat, who wrote in 1850 that plunder could be identified by seeing "if the law benefits one citizen at the expense of another by doing what the citizen himself cannot do without committing a crime." Tariffs empower the influential to sell their goods not on the basis of merit or price, but by means of State bullying, while the accompanying currency wars allow the influential to profit by the debasement of the people's purchasing power. It may be legalized plunder, but it is plunder nonetheless.

It is not just one country that falls prey to the illusion of getting rich by destroying the value of its money. Each wants the cheapest currency and is willing to print its money in whatever quantity is necessary to achieve that devalued status.

This is where we find the world today. Nations are in a race to devalue their money. And thus, currency wars—one manifestation of trade wars—are born. Currency wars are harbingers of larger trade wars to come, just as trade wars themselves are often preludes to hot wars.

This isn't the world's first modern currency war.

In his 2011 book, *Currency Wars: The Making of the Next Global Crisis*, James Rickards identifies three global currency wars in less than a century.

Currency War I (1921–1936)

The fuel for the first modern currency war was the end of World War I and the unpayable sovereign debt that the Treaty of Versailles saddled Germany with. The creation of the Federal Reserve in 1913 added another dynamic to the combustible mix, but the currency war itself was ignited by Weimar Germany's hyperinflation in 1921, followed by the collapse of the French franc in 1923. The later collapse of Austria's Credit Anstalt bank set off a banking panic in 1931, and serial currency devaluations soon swept Europe. The Great Depression quickly went global.

Across the Atlantic, FDR joined in, cheapening the dollar by nationalizing the people's gold and raising its price from $20.67 an ounce to $35. In doing so, he devalued the dollar by 60 percent, and put Americans on a paper money standard, a currency that could easily be further devalued at the pleasure of the trade warriors.

In Rickards's telling, "What followed after 1936 was not a continuation of a currency war but the bloodiest real war in history."

Currency War II (1967–1987)

The stage was set for Currency War II with President Johnson's fiscally reckless "guns and butter" policy, the combined spending for the Vietnam War and his Great Society. But it was the British pound sterling crisis in 1967 that triggered the war. That crisis, writes Rickards, was "the first major currency devaluation since Bretton Woods," referring to the global monetary structure agreed to by the western Allies after World War II.

The pivotal event of Currency War II was President Nixon's abandonment of the US dollar's ties to gold in 1971. That devaluation was accompanied by an additional 10 percent surtax on everything imported into the US, amounting to an additional de facto devaluation of the dollar.

Those decisions, along with Fed's monetary management of unprecedented volatility, led to a decade of economic stagnation characterized by three recessions, the quadrupling of oil prices, and a 50 percent plunge in the value of the dollar. It drove the first two gold bull markets described in the Introduction: the first as it helped push gold up to nearly $200 an ounce in 1974; and the second, as gold raced to $850 an ounce in January 1980.

Rickards's account of Currency War II ends with the Plaza Accord of 1985 and a follow-up agreement, the Louvre Accord of 1987. The arrangement devalued the dollar sharply against the German mark, the French franc, and the Japanese yen. It was all a predictable failure, accompanied in the US by slow growth (3.2 percent in 1987), high unemployment (7 percent in 1986), and high inflation (which eventually edged up to 6.1 percent in 1990).

Currency War III (2010–)

The mortgage meltdown and the Panic of 2008 marked the prelude to Currency War III, which was underway in earnest by 2010. It threatens to end the dollar's post-World War II reign as the world's reserve currency. Like Currency Wars I and II, it will debauch the purchasing power of the dollar and other paper currencies. And, like the prior currency wars, it will drive the price of gold to new highs.

This war threatens to be much bigger than the last two. Rickards says Currency War III "...will be truly global and fought on a more massive scale than ever.... Today the risk is not just of devaluation of one currency against another or a rise in the price of gold. Today the risk is the collapse of the monetary system itself—a loss of confidence in paper currencies and a massive flight to hard assets. Given these risks of catastrophic failure, Currency War III may be the last currency war."

The road to disorder has just begun, concludes Rickards.

Currency wars, like trade wars, can quickly escalate with serial devaluations and targeted retaliations. As is the case in trade wars, if foreigners no longer sell goods to US customers, they no longer have dollars to buy the products made by American workers.

The race to destroy the purchasing power of the world's major currencies is just getting started. It won't create more prosperity; it will only redistribute a diminishing prosperity to the crony classes.

It will, however, succeed in destroying today's paper dollar. Just as no one measures fabric with a shrinking yardstick, or gasoline by a gallon of diminishing size, the dollar's role as a measure of value and a standard of commerce will fail and the dollar price of gold will become irrelevant. No longer will you measure the value of your gold in dollars but rather by how many ounces or grams that you own.

When the State embarks on an explicit policy of destroying the value of its currency, it will no doubt succeed in doing so. Under such circumstances, one should cash out of that currency in favor of a currency of enduring value, one not subject to the manipulation of lunatics.

CHAPTER 4

THE WAR ON CASH

Whose Picture Is on that Money?

You have never met a more cocksure lot than the monetary-policy clerisy.

—James Grant

Cash Is Trash

As the global trade war grows, there is another State menace, the fourth on our list, that will provide a powerful blow to the State's currency. It is the war on cash. The State's war on cash has been low-grade until now. However, with bothersome reporting requirements, the criminalization of and ceilings on allowable cash transactions, and prohibitions on the transportation of cash, as well as efforts to stop the production and use of $100 bills, it is picking up momentum and may soon come roaring its meddlesome way into the financial lives of average Americans.

Federal Reserve officials, along with former treasury secretary Larry Summers and former International Monetary Fund (IMF) chief economist Kenneth Rogoff (both with Harvard

University), are among those pushing hard for a much more aggressive war on cash. In fact, Rogoff authored a recent book called *The Curse of Cash,* arguing that cash must be eliminated altogether to further empower the State's monetary authorities.

Trump has not spoken directly about the war on cash, but it is contiguous with State activities that find favor in his authoritarian outbursts, such as his off-the-cuff call for a boycott of Apple Inc. when it resisted the FBI's demand for encryption-breaking access to iPhones, or his casual and equally uninformed support for civil asset forfeiture. In any case, there is no evidence to suggest Trump will resist this objective of the Deep State.

Generally, when people are found standing in lines to buy gold, it is during a full-blown crisis. They are desperate to exchange their failing paper money for enduring wealth. (To repeat an earlier observation, no one has ever reported a case of people lining up anxious to exchange their gold for paper money.) But as 2020 got underway, people in Germany could be found standing in queues to buy gold. This time it wasn't because the Euro was in free fall. Instead, they were reacting to another attack on cash.

The German government was adopting measures to criminalize anyone buying gold anonymously in amounts of 2,000 euros or more. The new provisions required that the identity of customers be recorded and demanded criminal background checks on businesses making such purchases. At the same time, precious metals dealers were required to report certain customers to the state authorities; failure to comply demanded stiff fines.

Governments are quickly tightening the screws on people trying to withdraw from the financial matrix. The threshold for Germany's intrusive reporting requirements, said to conform to European Union standards, had dropped rapidly from 15,000 euros in 2017 to 10,000. But it was lowering the limit to 2,000 euros that triggered people to stand in line to beat the new law. One poster on social media wrote, "They don't want normal people to bank run their scam paper… They want to know every single person that tries to get out of their cage."

Elements of the War of Cash

A war on cash in the US is really a war on financial privacy. It empowers state surveillance in a way that the worst totalitarian regimes of history could only have wished. Eliminating the anonymity of cash transactions allows the tracking of nonconforming behavior. It is a necessary policy tool of authoritarian thought control programs like the Social Credit System that China's ruling party ramped up in 2018. The Social Credit System creates digital profiles of people, ranking their loyalty, trustworthiness, and compliance with the aims of the State, creating blacklists as a means of suppressing dissent and dissenters.

Early on in the US, the State captured important territory in the war on cash with the Bank Secrecy Act of 1970. It requires that financial institutions report all deposits, withdrawals, exchanges, or transfers of currency of more than $10,000 to the government. The required "currency transaction report" must also be filed in the event of multiple transactions that amount to more than the $10,000 threshold.

Likewise, people carrying, transporting, or shipping currency, traveler's checks, or other instruments of more than $10,000 out of the country must report it to the government. Those with foreign accounts, including securities accounts, or authority over a foreign account of more than $10,000 must also file a report with the Treasury Department.

Banks are also required to maintain a log of those who purchase money orders, cashier's checks, and traveler's checks totaling $3,000 to $10,000. These logs must be maintained for five years.

There is even an Orwellian requirement for banks to file a " suspicious activity report" on those who may simply appear to be trying to avoid the annoyance of the State's reporting requirements, whether they have actually done so or not. To make it all the more creepy, the bank is forbidden to tell its customers when it is filing a suspicious activity report about them.

There is even a related crime called "structuring," which involves managing financial transactions in a manner designed to avoid reporting requirements.

These cash reporting laws have victimized innocent people from all walks of life, those otherwise under no suspicion of criminality: A dairy farmer in Maryland had his bank account with $70,000 seized because he had been making bank deposits under $10,000. There was no question that the money had been earned legitimately. A bank teller had simply advised him that deposits of more than $10,000 would be a reporting nuisance. A couple given cash at a traditional Greek wedding was busted for making a series of small deposits because they didn't want to wait in line filling out paperwork.

Over the years, the intrusion has wormed its way down into smaller and smaller transactions. The reporting threshold today remains at $10,000, an amount that in constant dollars would have been the equivalent of demanding the reporting of transactions of only $1,500 in 1970 when the law was passed. Along the way, the definition of financial institutions has been broadened to include auto dealers, jewelers, coins dealers, pawn shops, and other businesses.

The banks, as the obvious beneficiaries of the war on cash, are helping out where they can. In 2015, Chase updated its safe deposit box lease agreement with this term: "You agree not to store any cash or coins other than those found to have a collectible value."

Meanwhile the war on cash is spreading around the globe. Cash transactions have become either banned or reportable events in France, Italy, Spain, Switzerland, Russia, Mexico, and many other countries.

Is it hard to understand why people would resent these reporting requirements? Is it difficult to understand why people would stand in line to protect the privacy of their financial records in an age of home invasions, identity theft, and the now common reports that businesses' customer credit card numbers and other records have been stolen? Just as common is the criminal breaching of government databases. Those who take steps to keep their business records private are only behaving prudently, even if they must stand in lines to do so.

Many people have assessed for themselves the risks of unwelcome events in these times. Some are concerned about the possibility of bank closings. Others believe that someday there could be a failure of the power grid and that without electricity,

ATMs will stop spitting out cash. Others remember when four thousand flights were grounded on the morning of September 11, 2001; they would like to protect themselves from the consequences of a large-scale terrorist event. Still others were denied access to their safe deposit boxes when bank branches closed during the 2020 coronavirus lockdown.

Whatever their reasons, in conducting their affairs with admirable prudence, they choose to keep a reserve of some cash. In doing so, they put themselves at odds with the Deep State and even local governments that use the war on cash as an opportunity to enrich themselves with something called "civil asset forfeiture." Our friend Mark Nestmann, whose company helps people secure second passports and other offshore strategies, explains:

> One strategy the government uses to discourage people from holding cash is civil forfeiture. Under this Alice-in-Wonderland legal process, cops can seize your cash—or anything else you own—if they believe that it's somehow connected to a crime...*any* crime. You don't need to be convicted, accused, or even arrested for a crime to lose everything you own....
>
> In a criminal proceeding, you have the right to be presumed innocent until a jury finds you guilty "beyond a reasonable doubt." If police seize your property in a civil forfeiture, it's "presumed guilty." It's up to you to prove that it's not associated with a crime. That's a tall order and a big reason why 80 percent of forfeiture cases go uncontested.

The procedural rules governing forfeiture cases are also very complex. Only a handful of attorneys are familiar with them, and they charge accordingly for this knowledge. The last time I checked, I couldn't find an attorney willing to help a client reclaim wrongfully seized property from police for a retainer under $20,000. If you're poor, like most victims of civil forfeiture, there's no way you'll be able to come up with the money to contest the seizure.

Civil asset forfeitures amount to billions of dollars each year. Abuses of an already abusive intrusion are rampant. Here is one example from a 2015 Heritage Foundation report: "In Detroit, Michigan, authorities raided a 'Funk Night' event at the Contemporary Art Museum and seized 40 cars from the 130 attendees on the theory that the attendees were somehow responsible for the fact that the organizers of the event had failed to obtain a permit to serve alcohol, and the cars had been used to transport them to the event."

All the charges were eventually dropped, but the victims still had to pay $900 to recover their impounded cars.

In a February 2017 White House meeting with county sheriffs from across the country, President Trump went on the record supporting civil asset forfeitures. When told there was a lot of pressure to end forfeitures, Trump asked, "Who would want that pressure, other than, like, bad people, right?"

India's Currency Call-In

The chaos of a war on cash was put on display in India in 2016 when the government demonetized or repudiated the most widely used currency units. Commerce in India is dependent on cash, where it is more widely used than in countries in which bank cards are common. The cash denominations repudiated, five hundred and 1,000-rupee banknotes, worth just under about $7.50 and $15 respectively, were the rough usage equivalent to $10 and $20 bills in the US and together represent 80 percent of the currency in circulation.

The sudden currency call-in was, of course, a tax grab sold as means of cracking down on "illegal cash" and fighting counterfeiting and corruption. Under the program, the old bills could be exchanged for new ones over a period of weeks after which they became worthless. The exchanges were closely monitored by the government, which helped itself to cash holdings that couldn't be "adequately" explained. As it sought to ferret out large cash holdings, people exchanging currency had their fingers stained with indelible ink so they couldn't show up again with additional currency to exchange.

The government also banned cash transactions of more than three hundred thousand rupees, about $4,500. India's economic growth took a sharp hit under the new policy; millions of jobs were lost in the disruption. Queues appeared everywhere, with long lines of people trying to get cash for their everyday needs. Angry mobs took to the streets.

The scheme produced turmoil in the daily life of the Indian people, especially the poor. For those who had some means, it was a monumental inconvenience. Banks shut down even as tens of millions lined up to swap their banned paper notes for new ones.

The government expected up to a third of the currency in circulation to have been criminally tainted and believed that it wouldn't be turned in. Instead, 99 percent of the rupees were exchanged. When the disruption failed to produce the expected windfall from the black market, prime minister Narendra Modi changed the rationale for the demonetization. He began emphasizing that his war on cash was about moving India into digital commerce and banking. Left out of the calculation were more than a billion people in India who had no internet access, or who lived in places where electricity was unreliable.

Driving people like cattle into politically compelled behaviors carries costs—for the people. Because there are no accommodations for digital transactions in many of India's traditional food marketplaces, the needless cash shortages spelled havoc in the daily lives of many. Even before the currency switch, Indians complained that bank fees were mysterious and even arbitrary, and yet the government's plan was to drive all the people of India, willing or not, into the banking system.

Lurking in the background of the debacle was the planning and plotting of the US Agency for International Development, which is often found furthering the Deep State's international ambitions. Perhaps the currency call-in was a test run for similar attacks on cash economies elsewhere. Like all grandiose, top-down monetary schemes, this one was ill-conceived not just in theory, but in implementation. The government hadn't even prepared enough new notes for the exchange. ATMs, cash-less, became worthless.

In addition to the expected tax windfall for the State, the cash crackdown was intended to drive people to institutionalize their wealth: keep it in banks and other accounts subject to State control. But the people are not the chattel property of the State. They have their own objectives and preferences, customs and habits, and *they are capable of changing their monetary practices when they deem it in their individual interests to do so.* Once Modi's demonetization and cash exchange were finished, people began returning, although in lesser numbers, to their traditional dependence on cash transactions.

The government of India has long warred on the Indian people's traditional preferences to own gold, which represents a threat to that State's money manipulators. In 2012, a central bank official lectured Indians to stay away from the metal: "The poor should never invest in gold, for whenever they have purchased gold, it either lands up in the temple or in the hands of the moneylender or, at the most, it may be given away during a daughter's marriage." (It was typically poor government investment advice: from April 2012 to April 2020 the gold price in rupees climbed 40 percent.)

In 2013, the Reserve Bank of India "asked" banks to stop allowing for credit card purchases of gold, including jewelry and ornaments. Shortly thereafter, the government hiked the tariff on imported gold coins and bars to 10 percent and on jewelry to 15 percent. This drove silver purchasing to new heights and produced an increase in gold smuggling.

Our advice to the 1.37 billion people of India: keep some cash on hand to buy pitchforks when you've had enough abuse.

The Cyprus Bail-In

An audacious operation in Cyprus may be a model for future asset seizures. It illustrates the motivation governments can have to keep citizens' money institutionalized. It was a midnight bank bailout, although it might better be called a bail-in. Instead of employing means more familiar to Americans since 2008, that is, taxation via money printing to bail out insolvent banks, the government of Cyprus simply plundered private bank accounts in the middle of the night to recapitalize the country's two largest banks.

As part of an ongoing bank rescue operation, on March 13, 2013, the European Central Bank and the International Monetary Fund (always an agent of the Deep State's global intrigue) demanded, and the government of Cyprus agreed, that the Cypriot banks would be closed, and private accounts frozen for midnight looting by the authorities.

The government sought to excuse the seizures partially on the grounds that as much as half of the banks' deposits belonged to foreigners, non-European Union residents. Of course, the news sparked a run on the banks and a dash for ATM machines. Too late. The banks were closed, and the ATMs weren't working.

Shareholders, bondholders, and depositors with accounts of 100,000 euros in the Bank of Cyrus were "levied" for 47.5 percent of their assets above that amount. Their seized deposits became bank equity.

Other venues, including Greece, have explored the idea of similar levies on their depositors by imposing a special tax on the withdrawal of cash.

Negative Interest Rates

There are many motives behind the war on cash, among them the Deep State's ever-present impulse to track, surveille, monitor, and control the people with the digital trail a cashless economy provides.

A cashless economy enables the authorities to enact and transmit its initiatives and changes in monetary policy instantly, without resistance or noncompliance from those independent of its institutions. The government can impose taxes on money, or restrict its expatriation and movement, in a way that is difficult to do in a cash economy.

There is another reason that the Deep State is accelerating the war on cash. Statists are busy engineering, and hope to be able to impose when they see fit, a negative interest rate regime. The ability to use cash as an alternative to institutionalized money is the biggest impediment to this perverse plan of guaranteed confiscation.

Negative interest rates mean that instead of the banks paying you interest on your deposits, the banks would be able to penalize you or charge you interest on your deposits. Stated differently, instead of accumulating interest, your deposit in the bank for a year of, say, $1,000 would return to you less than that, perhaps $950 at the end of the period.

The Money Manipulators know perfectly well that, given a choice, no one will deposit money with them or the institutions they rule under those circumstances. Well, then, the people must not be given a choice! They must be herded and corralled into banking institutions by the elimination of cash.

Commerce outside of the banking institutions must be minimized and criminalized.

Bank robbers wear masks, tie people up, and use guns because people don't like being robbed. But as long as the governing classes are able to disguise their robbery as "monetary policy," or get away with the use of occult terms like "liquidity operations," "repurchase agreements," "demand management," or "quantitative easing," they are able to pass unmolested in polite company.

Other than a venal larceny, do the Deep State Money Manipulators provide any intellectual cover for their negative interest rate scheme? Of course they do. It is the same old Keynesian nonsense responsible for the condition of the dollar and the enormity of the debt: negative interest rates will allow them to stimulate demand by encouraging consumers to spend money at once, before their principal is depleted by the negative rate.

This rationale is made explicit in a 2017 IMF working paper, "The Macroeconomics of De-Cashing": "In particular, the negative interest rate policy becomes a feasible option for monetary policy if savings in physical currency are discouraged and substantially reduced. With de-cashing, most money would be stored in the banking system, and, therefore, would be easily affected by negative rates, which could encourage consumer spending."

Whether domestic or international, the statist economists are of one view: that consumption—spending—is the key to prosperity. History and common sense teach otherwise, that production must precede consumption, and that capital formation—savings or deferred consumption—is the surest means to increased production.

Among the enemies of cash is former Treasury Secretary Summers. He has penned pieces for the *Financial Times* and *Washington Post* arguing for the elimination of large bills in both Europe and the United States. Although the American people like it and use it, Summers wants the $100 bill eliminated. He shares Rogoff's argument in *The Curse of Cash* and hopes to tarnish people's desire to hold cash by linking it with criminality.

Rogoff writes that a lot of dollars and euros are held "in tax evaders' attics and drug dealers' closets." That may be true, but if there are already underlying crimes, tax evasion and drug dealing, why should the holding of cash be criminalized as well, sweeping up people not guilty of those underlying offenses? After all, even the charts Rogoff provides show a clear bump in currency holdings coinciding with the risk and insolvency of state-chartered banks around the time of the Meltdown of 2008. With his war on cash, Rogoff, a chess grandmaster before he was an economist, would checkmate people who are merely trying to protect themselves from the systemic risk of bank insolvency.

Rogoff argues along with most cash opponents that a cashless system, or at least one with nothing larger than a $10 bill, allows the Money Manipulators to "manage" and "stabilize" the economy. This is so farcical, given the mismanagement and destabilizing performance history of the Money Manipulators discussed in chapter 1, that it hardly needs to be refuted.

Rogoff even recommends replacing small bills with bulky, inconvenient coins to make carrying large quantities of cash more burdensome. This inconvenience-by-design raises fundamental questions about Rogoff's and Summers' underlying philosophy: does the State's monetary system exist to serve the people? Or does the monetary system exist to serve the State in its drive to control the people? It is really an age-old philosophical question: Does the State itself exist to serve the people? Or do the people exist to serve the State?

The State's answer is obvious. That is why it wants everything *it* does to remain a secret, while it wants everything *you* do to be an open book. To keep its eye on you it must do away with commercial transactions that go unrecorded. It is not willing to let anyone escape its monetary oversight or its tax authorities.

Driven by statist economics, a group called the Independent Commission for the Reform of International Corporate Taxation proposed in 2018 the use of block chain technology to create a global wealth registry. Its objective is to combat wealth inequality and financial secrecy and to facilitate tax collection. The proposal includes the registry of "tangible and intangible assets" worth $10,000 or more. It targets real estate, gold, art or cash, financial securities of every kind, and even intellectual property. Like other war-on-cash initiatives, it underscores gold's virtue as the financial asset least vulnerable to the State's hunger for control.

Nobody should have been surprised by the midnight bank bail-in in Cyprus. Or to find the agents of the US Deep State in the background of India's currency call-in. As deficits grow and debts pile up, the less trustworthy the State's money becomes; the more aggressively it experiments with and propagates punitive measures that force reliance on it; and the more intrusively and suspiciously it behaves. The more harebrained its proposals, the more clearly it telegraphs its future actions.

As the State cracks down on cash, it drives alert people to take their wealth out of the system.

The war on cash will prompt growing numbers to buy gold. It is an accelerant of *The Last Gold Rush…Ever.*

Never Forget

Take a good look at whose face is on the US currency in your pocket. The notes, except for Benjamin Franklin on the $100 bill, all feature former presidents. It's the same with the coins. The other images, the buildings (the White House, the Treasury Building, the Lincoln Memorial, the Capitol Building), seals, and signatures are all those of the State.

When asked about taxation two thousand years ago, Jesus asked in return whose image was on the coinage. It was Caesar's. It was the State's money then. The currency remains the State's money today. While people believe the money is theirs, in fact the State thinks otherwise. The State believes that it can confiscate, inflate, devalue, nationalize, and demonetize *its* money whenever it wishes.

It can. It does.

It is the State's money.

CHAPTER 5

THE NEW WORLD ORDER

Or Is It the Old One?

While history runs its course, it is not history to us. It leads us into an unknown land, and but rarely can we get a glimpse of what lies ahead.

—Friedrich Hayek

The Strain and the Choke Chain

When the late senator John McCain complained that the "New World Order" is under enormous strain, he was only half right. The strain is very real, but it belongs to the old, not a new world order. The architecture of a new order is so far undelineated; there is not an inevitable new paradigm struggling to be born. Instead, the strain he described is in the decline of the post-World War II order of US global economic hegemony, geopolitical dominance, and America's Global Military Empire. It will leave a vacuum to be filled, perhaps as great as that left by the collapse of the ancient Roman world.

Conventional politicians from McCain and Bush to Obama and Hillary Clinton have ranged from partially to totally clueless about the breakdown of the modern-day Wilsonian fantasy of a grand US global hegemony. Each has been a tool of the Deep State's interest in preserving the status quo, a world order of US foreign adventurism, global standoffs, and money manipulation, all conducted with the American taxpayer serving as its milk cow. The fantasy had lost its luster with the public before: after the deadly debacle that was World War I; after the carnage of Vietnam; and now, as the resonance of Donald Trump's 2016 campaign rhetoric made clear, in the aftermath of the Iraq misadventure. Trump on the stump seemed willing to surge forward and sever ties with conventions and institutions that belong to the fading order. As president-elect, Trump was explicit about the difference to expect from his foreign policy: "We will stop racing to topple foreign regimes that we know nothing about, that we shouldn't be involved with." Sadly, the president appears to have surged forward into the past, another captive of the Deep State.

So fixed are the institutional presumptions of the "Old World Order" foreign policy, that Trump repeatedly found his attempts to change them thwarted by his own staff. No sooner had the president announced in 2018 that the US was leaving Syria (the *Guardian* reported that Trump ordered "a full, rapid withdrawal") than national security advisor John Bolton and secretary of state Mike Pompeo answered with a tug on the president's leash, announcing that "leaving" didn't actually mean leaving. Robert Merry, an editor of the *American Conservative*, also sees a hidden hand at work in Trump the president's departure from Trump the candidate. If time and again Trump has abandoned his foreign policy promises, it may be because he encountered the power of the Deep State in Russiagate. "It appears now that the Mueller investigation has given him a sharp pull on his choke chain, which has generated a certain docility on his leash," Merry says. Of Trump's National Security Statement, released at the end of his first year, in December 2017, Merry writes:

> [T]his National Security Strategy does little to pull America away from the impulses and concepts that have guided US foreign policy since the end of the Cold War. The global hegemonic ambition, the interference with Russia in its own neighborhood, the NATO push eastward, the bellicosity toward Iran and ambition to remake the Middle East, the ongoing US military footprint in that region, the ongoing Afghan adventure, the embrace of Israeli and Saudi regional ambitions, the commitment to the obsolete NATO mission—all emerge as pillars of the Trump foreign policy, just as they have been pillars of US policy since 9/11. Trump has been coopted—if indeed he ever possessed any serious intention of changing America's direction in the world.

Implicit in the militarism of Trump's personnel choices and budget priorities is a fidelity to the myth of full-spectrum American dominance; the monetary and managed trade policies he supports suggest he believes that a return to the era of unparalleled American economic might is still possible. One may correctly lament the displacement of America's economic juggernaut—it would not have happened but for the squandering of American capital and freedom in an orgy of government growth—but, nevertheless, American global hegemony is a thing of the past.

Having to one degree or another cast off the rule of their communist and socialist dogmas, countries like China, India, and even Vietnam, to say nothing of those in eastern Europe, have moved into the twenty-first century and become productive, diminishing the relative economic might of the US. (At the same time, in a weird sort of compensation, the US is embracing the socialism of those countries' pasts, something that will be discussed in more detail in the following chapter.) Meanwhile, the dollar's role in world trade is changing with the rise of economic competitors, and because it is no longer anchored to gold, these changes do not spell greater value and strength for the dollar.

Sensing the shifting circumstances, the rest of the world is doing the heretofore unthinkable: it is moving into open defiance of the US, resisting its priorities, bowing out of its sanctions regimes, and, frankly, ignoring its diplomatic demands. Examples include the raucous 2018 G-7 Summit in Canada, described by the BBC as having "ended in acrimony."

Not only have US interventions in Afghanistan, Iraq, Libya, and Syria made conditions in each much worse and radicalized entire populations, they have discredited the US and the very idea of a unipolar world. Apprehensive about America's elective warfare, in 2005 longtime rivals Russia and China conducted their first ever joint military exercises. Russia, China, and Iran entered 2020 conducting joint naval exercises.

Although each of these three faces of the US postwar era— its economic hegemony, geopolitical dominance, and global military empire—are interdependent, we will examine the economic and geopolitical factors in turn. The ending of the American military Empire is so dispositive that it will be separately addressed, fittingly, in the final chapter, *The Empire's End.*

Economic Power

"The American Century" refers to an era that began with the end of World War II. While much of the industrial world's manufacturing had been bombed back in time, the US emerged relatively unscathed as the world's manufacturing hegemon. Today, with American economic hegemony rapidly slipping away, the American Century looks to fall short of a full hundred years.

Evidence can be found in wage stagnation. The real wages of most US workers are little changed or lower since the 1970s. Increasing evidence shows the long-term decline of US manufacturing dominance. The US was responsible for 29 percent of the world's "manufacturing value added" as recently as the early 1980s. By 2014, that had fallen to 17 percent.

The recent growth story is this: Almost six million Americans lost manufacturing jobs between 2000 and 2010. By the end of that decade, in 2010, China surpassed the US for the first time in global manufacturing. The Manufacturing Institute reports that between 2000 and 2012, the US share of manufactured goods exports fell in half, from 18 percent to 9 percent, while China's share tripled over the same period, from 6 percent to 18 percent. US manufacturing has been growing more slowly over the last decade than that of China, Japan, Germany, and even Mexico.

Look beyond manufacturing.

China's share of global GDP growth in 2000 was 7.42 percent. Its 2019 share is estimated at 27.2 percent. Over the same period, the US share has slipped from 20.76 percent to 12.3 percent. By many estimates China's GDP will surpass that of the US in a dozen years or fewer.

De-Dollarization

Among the most vulnerable elements in the fading Old World Order is the US dollar's role as the world's reserve currency. In that capacity, conferred on it under the postwar Bretton Woods agreement, foreign governments and central banks hold dollars (as they once did gold) against which they issue their own currencies; accordingly, the dollar has served as the key currency used in the global commodities trade and in settling international accounts. The foreign exchange markets trade as much as $6.6 trillion a day; the dollar figures in nine out of ten transactions.

Meanwhile, the dollar holdings of these central banks and governments represent 62 percent of the world's currency reserves. That is almost $6.8 trillion that has provided an underpinning for the dollar's value, a support that will erode as the dollar's reserve role wanes.

Those trillions of foreign reserve dollars are effectively a claim on the goods and services of America. As foreign banks dishoard those dollars, at a moderate pace for now but at an accelerating rate in a crisis, they will come flooding back home and bid up prices in the American economy just as surely as if they were newly printed dollars dropped from helicopters.

Just because foreign nations and their internal money manipulators are willing to fleece the people of their lands with their own irredeemable printed currencies doesn't mean they are willing to be fleeced by ours. Most of them are very aware of the dangerous monetary and debt games being played by the US. None of them want to be left holding the old maid in a dollar crisis. Accordingly, in 2009 China and Russia called for the creation of a new international currency, one diversified away from any individual nation and its monetary malpractice. No doubt the prospect of the US unilaterally freezing dollar accounts held in foreign banks and the threat of being banned from the dollar payment system—as is Iran—are also upper-most in their minds.

Around the world, central banks are furiously creating non-dollar trading and settlement initiatives to protect them-selves from devaluation, inflation, and US sanctions. In March 2017, Russia's central bank opened on office in Beijing and is preparing to issue Russian bonds denominated in Chinese yuan, while China intends to reciprocate, issuing ruble-denom-inated bonds. The *South China Morning Post* says the move is "widely viewed as intended to 'dethrone' the US dollar."

At the same time, and most significantly for our purposes, the World Gold Council reports that central banks are acquiring gold at the fastest rate since the US broke the dollar's last link to gold in 1971. China and Russia figure prominently in the move, as they convert their dollar reserves into gold. Both countries are clearly wondering why they should support US imperialism and bellicosity on their own frontiers by buying US bonds. Not much longer will they remain enablers of US saber-rattling and militarism.

China's official gold reserves have grown dramatically since 2000, from 395 metric tons to 1,948 tons in the second quarter of 2020. No less serious is Russia about building its gold reserves, which climbed from 343 to 2,292 tons over the same period. A Bank of Russia official explains that fortifying their gold reserves provides both diversification and protection against legal and political risks.

These moves, as substantial as they are, merely foreshadow the coming stampede of *The Last Gold Rush…Ever.*

At the same time, the centers of global gold trading are shifting to the East, from New York, London, and Zurich to Dubai, Singapore, Hong Kong, and Shanghai. This is wholly a market phenomenon, matching a subterranean river of precious metals that is flowing from private hands in the West to those in the East. Nations and people that are net acquirers of gold rise in the affairs of mankind. Those that are dishoarders decline. The future-shaping significance of this trend must not be dismissed.

Geopolitical Dominance

Trump's centerpiece 2016 campaign slogan, "Make America Great Again," was a frank acknowledgement of declining American preeminence. The decline can be illustrated in many ways. During the development of President Obama's Iran nuclear initiative, the Joint Comprehensive Plan of Action, it became clear that no matter what the US Congress did, Europe, China, and Russia would not abide the continuation of the US-driven sanctions regime on Iran, just as Europe has resisted US sanctions on Russia. When European leaders arranged talks with Russia and other parties to quell the fighting in Ukraine, the 2015 Minsk II talks, the US was pointedly not invited.

Meanwhile Britain, Germany, France, and others have joined China in the founding of the Asian Infrastructure Investment Bank, despite US squawking.

Meanwhile, at a hastily arranged Warsaw conference in February 2019 purportedly about Middle East security, vice president Mike Pence and secretary of state Mike Pompeo were effectively snubbed when European and other invitees sent lower-level diplomats. Israeli prime minister Benjamin Netanyahu let the cat out of the bag when he sent a tweet from the conference saying that the conference was "to advance the common interest of war with Iran."

US efforts to force Europe to cut economic ties with Iran and demand adherence to its sanctions regimes only spurs the development of sanctions-evading financial channels that circumvent US-dominated institutions. The US has "weaponized" the dollar; foreign nations react predictably to being bullied or bludgeoned by their dependence on the dollar in global trade. The growth of alternatives—channels that bypass US dominance and control—though slow to develop, will hasten the end of the world's reliance on the dollar as an indispensable reserve currency.

The BRICS nations—Brazil, Russia, India, China and South Africa—represent more than 41 percent of the world's population and together have a GDP greater than that of the US. The International Monetary Fund estimates the BRICS will account for 50 percent of global GDP by 2030. These nations have gathered in annual summits since 2009, banding together for political and economic cooperation as a reaction to US unipolarity. At the 2017 BRICS conference in China, Russian president Vladimir Putin's comments were transparent:

"Russia shares the BRICS countries' concerns over the unfairness of the global financial and economic architecture, which does not give due regard to the growing weight of the emerging economies. We are ready to work together with our partners to promote international financial regulation reforms and to overcome the excessive domination of the limited number of reserve currencies."

The end of the Old World Order is the fifth converging reason for *The Last Gold Rush...Ever.* Waning US economic dominance, especially the vulnerability of the dollar's position as the reserve currency of the world, and the accompanying geopolitical isolation of the US are powerful accelerants for gold in two ways.

First, during the financial crisis of 2008, many nations complained about US management of the dollar. A demand for reform by the governor of the People's Bank of China, published by the Bank for International Settlements in 2009, called for a super-sovereign reserve currency not susceptible to the manipulation by a single nation-state. It is a common complaint and echoes the critique of the dollar standard by French president Charles de Gaulle as far back as 1965: "We hold as necessary that international exchange be established...on an indisputable monetary base that does not carry the mark of any particular country.... Yes, gold, which does not change in nature, which is made indifferently into bars, ingots and coins, which does not have any nationality, which is considered, in all places and at all times, the immutable and fiduciary value par excellence."

Gold is the super-sovereign currency, one not susceptible to manipulation by a single nation. As the dollar standard deteriorates, the underpinning that privilege has provided to the dollar's exchange value must slip. With this loss of its purchasing power (and, accordingly, an incremental decline in the standard of living of the American people), the dollar price of gold will rise.

Second, as the global economic center of gravity shifts from Washington and reserves of foreign nations and their central banks are diversified out of the dollar, other currencies or baskets of currencies will replace them in central banking systems. Certainly, central bank reserve demand for gold, "the immutable and fiduciary value par excellence," will play an important role in that diversification, further propelling its price and driving the dollar gold rush. These moves will represent a *de facto* remonetization of gold.

To See Ourselves

Ron Paul is duly concerned that when the US does have a real economic or currency crisis, instead of assistance or cooperation in its time of need, "there will be a lot of piling on by the rest of the world."

It is a profound observation, one that would shock most Americans who have no idea what the US does on the world stage. It is impossible to know just how the backlog of anti-US resentment might play out, so rather than try to predict, we want to use the rest of this chapter on America's place in the larger world to describe some of the Deep State's global activities. These activities, which are little known by the American people, are well-known by people elsewhere. It is intended to suggest the speed and intensity with which the rest of the world may lock arms against the US, and the powerful forces that can motivate the "piling on" in a crisis and, therefore, drive gold as an alternative to the dying, Old World Order of dollar hegemony.

Few Americans would recognize the hand of the Deep State in something as benign sounding as the National Endowment for Democracy (NED).

The NED is a Washington-based nonprofit organization with congressional funding in the neighborhood of $170 million a year. Its annual report for 2014, the year that it was complicit in "regime change" in Ukraine, lists eighty-four separate projects and initiatives, mostly election-centered, that it plied with grants of hundreds of thousands of US tax dollars. The descriptions of these interventionist projects are laden with the same bureaucratic, statist jargon ("outreach," "mobilize," "engagement") that characterize power-seeking, tax-hungry groups in the US: *To bolster cross-regional, coalition-led advocacy...to strengthen and support civic initiatives... stimulate informed debate and dialogue.... To foster civic engagement...*

None of this discloses what the National Endowment for Democracy has really been up to in places like Ukraine and elsewhere. Advocacy? Of what? Dialogue? To what end? Mobilize? Who? Such questions matter, since no serious person thinks that all reforms, initiatives, and engagements are constructive. Reform? In pursuit of what? What civic initiatives? Which engagements? Who are the recipients of this money and what political objectives travel silently under benign-sounding cover?

Before looking for answers to these questions, it should be sufficient to simply ask what Americans would think if a hostile superpower halfway around the world busied itself funding scores of engagements, initiatives, and political advocacy groups in a neighboring country. Is it really difficult to imagine how Americans would react to China undertaking such interventions in Mexico or Canada?

Since the NED's annual report and its language are crafted to appear benign, we must look elsewhere to find evidence of the objectives behind the NED's taking sides in elections and partisan issues around the world, and sometimes even taking careful steps to conceal its role as the funder of secret foreign interventions. On inspection it is clear that the goal of the NED is service to the American Global Military Empire.

The evidence is available for anyone willing to look. With the stunning disclosures of the criminal activities of the CIA by the Church Committee and others in the 1970s, an effort was made to sanitize the agency's foreign meddling, shifting its funding activities in 1983 to the new and benevolent-sounding National Endowment for Democracy. One of the founders of the NED, historian Alan Weinstein, said in 1991, "A lot of what we do today was done covertly twenty-five years ago by the CIA."

That point was made succinctly in a July 2015 *Consortium News* column by the late investigative reporter Robert Parry. He describes the NED as a distinct successor to certain CIA activities:

> [The] NED is a US government-funded organization created in 1983 to do what the Central Intelligence Agency previously had done in financing organizations inside target countries to advance US policy interests and, if needed, help in "regime change."

The secret hand behind NED's creation was CIA Director William J. Casey, who worked with senior CIA covert operation specialist Walter Raymond Jr. to establish NED in 1983. Casey...focused on creating a funding mechanism to support groups inside foreign countries that would engage in propaganda and political action that the CIA had historically organized and paid for covertly. To partially replace that CIA role, the idea emerged for a congressionally funded entity that would serve as a conduit for this money.

But Casey recognized the need to hide the strings being pulled by the CIA. "Obviously we here [at CIA] should not get out front in the development of such an organization, nor should we appear to be a sponsor or advocate," Casey said in one undated letter to then-White House counselor Edwin Meese III—as Casey urged creation of a "National Endowment."

Since the CIA thought it wise to use the American people's money to subsidize socialist and left-wing unions and similar ideological groups, and even literary journals to manipulate policies and interfere in elections around the world during the first Cold War, one should view with great skepticism its funding successor's activities today. As it happens, the NED is much more concerned with tilting elections than with "democracy."

The head of the NED has made clear its current objective involves destabilizing the Russian government. This is the hubris of the Sorcerer's Apprentice, conjuring up dangerous forces under the illusion that outcomes are—despite all experience to the contrary—both predictable and controllable. Such interventionism's track record is impressive only in its failures. Judging from results in places like Iran, Vietnam, Iraq, Libya, and Syria where the Empire has set in motion coups and regime changes, one fairly shudders to think what atavistic forces they are capable of setting loose in the disintegration of Russia, home not so very long ago of show trials, the Lubyanka prison, Siberian gulags, and the murderous Joseph Stalin.

Despite their stunning record of failure, the hubris of the Deep State meddlers remains breathtaking. In serial *Washington Post* pieces, Carl Gershman, head of the NED since 1984, makes clear that Putin is his target for regime change, and Ukraine is "the biggest prize." Gershman urges more US "engagement" with Ukraine, Georgia, and Moldova while he complains of Russian "bullying" with "economic threats and trade sanctions."

With that, Gershman reveals a profound psychological blind spot since it is the US Empire that uses economic threats and trade sanctions more than any other country in the world. Such threats are the chief tool of its foreign policy; it relies on the bludgeoning of sanctions as an ever-ready substitute for diplomacy. In 2015, the US had in place both targeted and comprehensive sanctions against twenty-eight countries. At the same time, the government maintains some fifty "states of national emergency." (Most Americans would be surprised to learn that President Obama declared a "State of Emergency" against Venezuela, as though Venezuela's economic failure represented an existential threat to the US.) The Treasury Department even has an Office of Foreign Assets Control to manage commercial prohibitions against some six thousand individuals, businesses, and groups.

In the same wobbly, one-sided way, Gershman responded bitterly when Russia, having had enough of outside destabilization efforts and the kinds of new foreign interventionism propaganda and electoral initiatives discussed in Congress, sent the NED packing and demanded that such organizations henceforth register as "foreign agents." Gershman responded in the *Washington Post*, complaining, "They know that these laws contradict international law, which allows for such aid, and that the laws are meant to block a better future for Russia."

However, the US itself requires the registration of foreign agents, and its laws expressly forbid foreign governments or their agents from any involvement in US elections.

Although the NED spends about $100 million a year on its foreign intrusions, that is only a part of more than $5 billion the US spent on so-called "democracy-building programs" in Ukraine since the Warsaw Pact ended and Ukraine became independent of the Soviet Union in 1991. Some of that money came from the US Agency for International Development (USAID). This is an agency long suspected in foreign capitals where it is active, and among others that follow its activities closely, of being a front for or an operational partner of the CIA.

The USAID describes itself as "an independent agency that provides economic, development, and humanitarian assistance around the world in support of the foreign policy goals of the United States." That description provides cover for a lot of political meddling. The organization's activities are thick with the crony cut-outs and the corruption typical of foreign aid schemes, even as it lines the pockets of foreign despots.

Headlines such as this one in 2015 from the *Washington Post* describing an Inspector General report on USAID should surprise no one: "Watchdog: US may have spent taxpayer dollars on Afghanistan schools that didn't exist." According to the story about ghost schools, ghost teachers, and ghost administrators, the current Afghan government under Ashraf Ghani claims the prior administration under Hamid Karzai lied to get more funding.

In 2017, US taxpayers spent $55 billion on USAID and State Department "discretionary funding." It is a figure that doesn't measure the subsequent demands for warfare and additional new spending in response to the chaos the interventionists uncork. American prosperity suffers the death of a thousand cuts with the money these agencies and initiatives bleed from the people, funding a multitude of bureaucratic schemes and counterproductive initiatives around the world. Such programs call to mind Ron Paul's observation that "foreign aid is taking money from poor people in rich countries to give to rich people in poor countries."

It shouldn't be necessary to point out that this busybody-ism is exactly the kind of activity that the America's founders warned the young American republic to avoid:

> *The great rule of conduct for us in regard to foreign nations is in extending our commercial relations, to have with them as little political connection as possible.... Why quit our own to stand upon foreign ground? Why, by interweaving our destiny with that of any part of Europe, entangle our peace and prosperity in the toils of European ambition, rivalship, interest, humor or caprice?*

> —George Washington, Farewell Address, 1796

CHARLES GOYETTE AND BILL HAYNES

Peace, commerce, and honest friendship with all nations, entangling alliances with none.

—Thomas Jefferson, First Inaugural Address, 1801

Wherever the standard of freedom and independence has been or shall be unfurled, there will her [America's] heart, her benedictions and her prayers be. But she goes not abroad in search of monsters to destroy. She is the well-wisher to the freedom and independence of all. She is the champion and vindicator only of her own.

—John Quincy Adams, July 4, 1821 Address

The rest of the world doesn't require a great deal of convincing that the US acts with imperial impunity around the world. It is behavior that engenders resentment.

Even among our putative allies.

In Germany, where the East German population had suffered forty years of State surveillance by the Communists, and the entire people by the Nazis before that, NSA eavesdropping cast the US as arrogant, power-hungry, and untrustworthy among large majorities. The German magazine *Der Spiegel,* which broke the news, described Germans as "scandalized" in learning of US spying on chancellor Angela Merkel's cell phone; it said the German government was "furious." Later it was learned that the US was spying on *Der Speigel* as well.

There is more to the resentment of the US than just the indignity of snooping on private phone calls. The US national surveillance State is engaged in industrial espionage—even on its allies.

Whistleblower Edward Snowden told German television viewers in January 2014 that NSA spying isn't limited to national security issues. "If there's information at Siemens that's beneficial to US national interests—even if it doesn't have anything to do with national security—then they'll take that information nevertheless," said Snowden.

Snowden's disclosures also revealed that the NSA engaged in industrial sabotage against Petrobras, the giant Brazilian oil company. The news was met with widespread resentment throughout Brazil.

It was for fear of such disclosures that the US was willing to employ heavy-handed means to apprehend Snowden—regardless of the resentment it was bound to provoke. In 2013, suspecting that Snowden was aboard, it arranged the grounding of an airplane carrying the president of Bolivia. Flying home to Bolivia from an energy conference in Russia, president Evo Morales's plane was suddenly denied access to airspace over France, Spain, and Italy. His flight had to be rerouted to Austria, where the plane was searched for Snowden.

To view such events objectively it is helpful to reverse roles. In the *Guardian*, John Pilger reframed the Evo Morales experience: "Imagine the aircraft of the president of France being forced down in Latin America on 'suspicion' that it was carrying a political refugee to safety—and not just any refugee, but someone who has provided the people of the world with proof of criminal activity on an epic scale."

Dictionary.com provides a rather benign first definition of the word *hegemony*: "leadership or predominant influence exercised by one nation over others..." But by the third definition, something is suggested of the way this leadership or predominance is viewed beyond the borders of the hegemon:

"(especially among smaller nations) aggression or expansionism by large nations in an effort to achieve world domination."

Americans should have learned something about the concept of *blowback* with the 9/11 attacks. Chalmers Johnson had warned beforehand of such a tragedy, adopting the CIA term. He made clear in his 2000 book *Blowback: The Costs and Consequences of American Empire,* that victims of the reaction to the hegemon's foreign meddling neither see it coming nor understand it when it happens. As he wrote after the tragedy, "The concept 'blowback' does not just mean retaliation for things our government has done to and in foreign countries. It refers to retaliation for the numerous illegal operations we have carried out abroad that were kept totally secret from the American public. This means that when the retaliation comes—as it did so spectacularly on September 11, 2001—the American public is unable to put the events in context."

This section warns of a different kind of blowback. It will be fueled by years of US imperialistic and lawless behavior around the world, and finally triggered by a critical mass of resentment of the US.

Among its manifestations will be a US that finds itself not just bereft of meaningful allies, but that it may find much of the rest of the world allied against it. Whether this plays out in military contexts depends on US overreach in the meantime and remains to be seen. What is certain is that this blowback will be experienced in the unwillingness of the rest of the world to continue funding US debt in any future financial crisis.

The reasons for the resentment of the rest of the world will remain a mystery to most Americans.

CHAPTER 6

BANANA REPUBLIC ECONOMICS

Lab Experiments

It doesn't matter how beautiful your theory is, it doesn't matter how smart you are. If it doesn't agree with experiment, it's wrong.

—Richard Feynman

Plantations of Plunder

The term "Banana Republic" was coined by famed short story writer O. Henry after time spent living in Central America. Actually, O. Henry (the pen name of William Sydney Porter) didn't just happen to "spend time" in Honduras. He fled there when he was facing federal charges of bank embezzlement in Austin, Texas, charges for which he eventually served three years.

Perhaps his firsthand familiarity with larceny provided O. Henry the facility to coin the term "banana republic." Although he used it somewhat offhandedly in his 1904 book *Cabbages and Kings,* it would become a living part of our language for its economical and evocative description of the way in which a small group of politically powerful cronies plunder a land and its people.

O. Henry's tale is set in the fictional land of Anchuria, although it easily could have been about Guatemala, Honduras, or other Central or South American nations exploited by a foreign commercial interest such as a fruit company, operating through a succession of generalissimos, caudillos, and colonels who, often at their own peril, fancy themselves to be the ones who are really in charge.

O. Henry probably never dreamed that his native land could itself become like Anchuria, controlled and plundered by a well-connected elite, a plutocracy and its cronies operating through a succession of interchangeable war-making presidents and congressional warlords, as easily as if the mighty United States were nothing more than a tiny flyspeck of a country.

This, the sixth economic contributor to *The Last Gold Rush...Ever*, is the indifference of the US to the lessons of banana republic economies. Chief among those lessons should be the currency calamities they enact time and again with unbacked, irredeemable, made-up paper and digital money. Like the monetary authorities of banana republics, the monetary authorities of the US are in charge of the quantity of their currency. And with that power they are following in the footsteps of the banana republics everywhere with their failed pesos, bolivars, sols, escudos, cruzeiros, and Zimbabwean "dollars."

A Fatherland? Or Toilet Paper?

It is not as though more laboratory experiments are needed in crazy statist monetary policies and crackpot economic theories. The experiments have already been conducted, not only in great powers like the Soviet Union and China, but in a host of dictatorships around the word. Today, Venezuela is like a living laboratory experiment, one we can see collapsing before our eyes.

Venezuela calls to mind Milton Friedman's most famous saying: "Put government in charge of the Sahara Desert, and in five years you'll have a shortage of sand."

What sand is to the Sahara, petroleum is to Venezuela. Venezuela has the largest oil reserves in the world. More than even Saudi Arabia. It has proved reserves of 297 billion barrels.

Then it happened. Venezuela, an oil exporter for almost a century, found it couldn't even meet its domestic oil needs. As president Hugo Chávez plundered oil revenue to buy popular support with government giveaways, investment in production suffered. At the same time, the expropriation of private assets drove away much-needed development capital. Venezuela had to become an oil importer. It was forced to import oil from places like Algeria and Russia to make an exportable blend. But then the money to pay for the foreign oil it needed ran out. Soon gasoline joined the list of Venezuela's other shortages: staples like soap and shampoo, rice and milk, coffee and sugar, and even toilet paper.

The consequences have been cruel, as the people are left without the basic goods that sustain life. Still, the foreign minister scolded the people, asking "What do you want, a fatherland or toilet paper?"

And yet the United States, defying all reason and experience, is emulating many of the same banana republic practices: deficit financing, state socialism, central economic planning, price controls, rationing, and hysterical levels of monetary expansionism or quantitative easing. As these policies ultimately destroy the value of fiat currencies, the demand for quality monetary alternatives like gold and silver skyrockets.

Eventually in broken and destitute Venezuela, an ounce of silver was enough to feed a family for months; an ounce of gold could pay off a house.

Life in Venezuela

Banana republic socialist Chávez, who died in 2013, and his designated successor, Nicolás Maduro, postured themselves and have been praised in the press as the champions of Venezuela's poor. Here is some of what they bequeathed the poor:

To get food to feed their families, thousands of the poor storm grocery stores. With the highest inflation rate in the world, prices fixed by the government below the cost of production insure empty store shelves. The government tracks the people to see that they are not buying too much of any item; President Maduro even instituted a program of mandatory fingerprinting at grocery stores to combat the widespread shortages that developed under his price control edicts. Phony prices posted in the stores are a cruel laughter at the people's plight since the necessities are not to be found.

A Fox News report said, "Defenders of the controls say that by keeping prices for basic goods artificially low, Venezuela helps the nation's poor lead more dignified lives."

There's dignity in being forced to give the Big Brother police State your fingerprints to buy food? And how much dignity is there in having to find primitive substitutes for toilet paper?

Always playing to the mobs, Maduro even told Venezuelans to loot the stores of a retail electronics chain that resisted the guaranteed losses of the State's price edicts. "Leave nothing on the shelves," Maduro exhorted the mobs.

Trashing the economy and spreading shortages and violence is not enough for Maduro. One of his moves was right out of George Orwell's *1984* with its Ministry of Truth and Ministry of Love. President Maduro created a "Ministry of Supreme Social Happiness." It sounds like a parody, but it's not.

In its annual rankings, Transparency International rated Venezuela among the most corrupt countries in the world, right up there with Iraq, Libya, and Afghanistan. It defines corruption as "the abuse of entrusted power for private gain." Maybe the hundreds of millions of Venezuelan oil dollars that government officials have stashed in private overseas accounts have something to do with the corruption rating. The fact that Chávez's daughter, Maria Gabriela Chávez, is a billionaire might factor in as well.

Starvation among Venezuelan children has mushroomed. A December 2017 *New York Times* story provided a moving account of hospitals overflowing with suffering children, grieving families, and inadequate resources:

> The Venezuelan government has tried to cover up the extent of the crisis by enforcing a near-total blackout of health statistics, and by creating a culture in which

doctors are often afraid to register cases and deaths that may be associated with the government's failures.

But the statistics that have come out are staggering. In the Ministry of Health's 2015 annual report, the mortality rate for children under 4 weeks old had increased a hundredfold, from 0.02 percent in 2012 to just over 2 percent. Maternal mortality had increased nearly fivefold in the same period.

When the Health Ministry provided a link to suppressed bulletins on the extent of infant mortality—a 30 percent increase in 2016 of the deaths of children under the age of one—the government removed the reports, fired the health minister, and put the army in charge of monitoring future bulletins.

The authors write of "years of economic mismanagement" in Venezuela. It would have been helpful if they had pointed out that the fault lies with the same socialist prescriptions the *New York Times* editorials regularly urge on the American people.

No one should be surprised that crime in Venezuela, including looting and murder, has skyrocketed, while the people are reduced to primitive bartering. Millions of people have fled the country, a million to Columbia alone where, *USA Today* reported in late 2018, "[A]t sunset each night, young Venezuelan women gather in Bolivar Plaza or by churches, looking to sell their bodies for sex."

Banana Republic Socialism

Venezuela's polices are the usual dog's breakfast of socialist governance: State socialism, economic interventionism, and central economic planning; suppression of property rights and monetary imbecility; redistributionism, taxation, and regulation; guaranteed income, empty health care promises, and welfarism; price controls, exchange controls, currency call-ins, and replacement schemes.

With an inflation rate that approached 500,000 percent annually in late 2018, the Venezuelan bolivar lost value by the minute, if not the second. The money printing cannot keep up with rising prices.

The almost worthless bolivar is the result of Venezuela's very own quantitative easing. The results have been all too predictable. Oil production has plummeted. With a worthless currency, the pipelines and refineries cannot keep their infrastructure in working order. With a worthless currency, farmers cannot buy feed, fertilizer, or anything else they need to be productive. So the people suffer. Some starve.

It doesn't take a generalissimo behind a pair of mirrored sunglasses, "scrambled eggs" splashed across the visor of a military hat, and a chest covered with the "fruit salad" of decorations to make a banana republic. Our warlords come dressed in suits and ties, the uniforms of the marbled halls of the capital city. The outer trappings may come and go, and the parties may follow one another in turn, just as the figures that serve as the face of the State can change, all without supplanting the Deep State oligarchy in the background.

As Murray Rothbard has written: "Economics is not concerned with the color of the uniform or with the good or bad manners of the rulers. Nor does it care which group or classes are running the State in various political regimes. Neither does it matter, for economics, whether the socialist regime chooses its rulers by elections or by *coups d'état*. Economics is concerned only with the powers of ownership or control that the State exercises."

Since the time of Karl Marx, socialism has been defined as ownership of the means of production in the hands of the State. But today, socialism is mostly practiced as a means of wealth redistribution and seen in the growth of the welfare and the crony state. It is implemented by the tax system without regard to nominal ownership of the means of production.

This is consistent with any modern banana republic, in which major industries, whether oil, banking, or health care, can be nationalized. Other businesses and individuals may remain the nominal owners of their property, although they may also be required to surrender it, or see their production and profits expropriated at any time.

At the heart of banana republics with their generalissimos in the third world, and the banana republics of the business suit and silk tie, is an eagerness to secure power and office by giving things to people to buy their support. Hugo Chávez, especially gifted at this shabby populism, was able to get away with it as long as record high oil prices could keep up with his spree of promises. America has gotten away with it on the momentum of the postwar prosperity and with the dollar's now-waning might.

Socialism is accompanied by an indifference to, or inability to account for, costs in the real world. Because it is a congenital defect among the political classes everywhere, there are as many examples of this economic insouciance in the first world as there are in the third world. A bipartisan pair of examples from Washington will illustrate.

A few years ago, President Obama announced an election year vote-buying goody for up to five million student loan borrowers. It was an executive decision to cap certain repayments.

The president (who, as related in chapter 2, didn't know the size of the US national debt) didn't know and couldn't say how much his new initiative would cost.

"We actually don't know the costs yet," education secretary Arne Duncan answered for the administration. "We'll figure that out on the back end."

On the back end.

Après nous.

Displaying the same financial indifference on the other side of the political divide and representing the syndrome from the legislative branch, senator Marco Rubio of Florida launched a proposal of his own at the same time, another Washington "big idea." (To qualify as a "big idea" in Washington, a scheme must involve substantial amounts of the people's money.) On the editorial page of the *Wall Street Journal*, Rubio called for the establishment of a "currency board" to prop up the value of the hryvnia, Ukraine's national currency. Rubio explained that Americans must extend to Ukrainians the benefits of having "a trustworthy sovereign currency."

Shouldn't the trustworthiness of Ukraine's money depend on Ukraine's fiscal and monetary probity? The world is crawling with countries that would like to have trustworthy sovereign currencies but are unwilling to act responsibly to get them. Why, then, should the American people, still straining under the "new normal" conditions of their own economy, be taxed to provide for Ukrainians what they are not willing to provide for themselves?

Often, to ingratiate themselves with influential patrons, politicians promote policies of the Deep State they don't really understand themselves. Does Rubio know exactly what a currency board is? It is not apparent in the text of his proposal. Like most grandiose banana republic schemes, this one didn't come with any hard and reliable figures attached. Rubio offered not a single number that would make clear the cost involved in funding a reserve sufficiently large to provide an unlimited liquid market for a broken currency at a fixed and artificially high price.

Ukraine is free to establish a rule-bound exchange rate using its own currency reserves, but Rubio had his eye on your money, citing IMF loans of unspecified scope. Of course, since the US is its largest contributor, the IMF is a Deep State device for laundering US taxpayer money.

Despite Ukraine's failure to meet the terms of two prior IMF loans, in 2014 the institution approved still another loan package, this time for $17.5 billion. In the air around these multinational deals one detects the scent of bankers desperate to be spared the risk of a default. A good chunk of the IMF funding package was approved to be used by Ukraine to pay banks and Gazprom, the Russian gas giant to which it owed billions.

So, to peel the onion: Americans sacrifice part of their livelihood to borrow money from foreign creditors like Russia (yes, Russia has been a significant creditor of the US) and China to launder through the IMF to give to Ukraine, which in turn will give the money to multinational banks and Russian plutocrats.

It's enough to bring a tear to your eye.

As a sidebar, President Trump closed out 2017 approving the sale of weapons to Ukraine. For those who wonder how Ukraine affords the arms, Daniel McAdams, executive director of the Ron Paul Institute, provides the familiar answer: "We give them money, they give it back to us, and they get weapons." A *Washington Post* story on the new arms sales concludes that "it's one sure sign that Trump's foreign policy views are evolving—or at least being influenced—as his presidency progresses."

Exactly.

Such measures, arming faraway countries in strictly local disputes and assuming financial liabilities in foreign countries, become the pretexts for drawing us into needless wars. These are the common means of the Deep State. It is much easier to sell foreign interventions to the American people if they have come to believe that they are inextricably involved in the affairs of a foreign state and are kept in the dark about the price they will be made to pay.

When Marco Rubio asks Americans to speculate in foreign currencies, one can only wonder how it is that any self-respecting editorial page editor at the nation's largest financial newspaper could approve a submission about a major financial initiative that is devoid of any meaningful financial information. Has the newspaper's ceaseless warmongering finally eclipsed its journalistic mission? If so, the *Wall Street Journal* has succumbed to the socialists' enmity for hard, real-world accounting, the bane of socialists of every stripe.

And what about our own currency? Has Senator Rubio looked at the fundamentals of the dollar?

It's enough to make a grown man cry.

Socialism in the US

The growth of socialism in the US can be seen in its individual programs: Social Security, Obamacare, Medicare, Medicaid, bank deposit insurance, farm and business subsidies and guarantees, government schools, corporate welfare, public transportation, government home loans and housing projects, government student loan programs, agricultural price fixing and farm support programs, to name just a few.

Especially offensive is the variant known as corporate capitalism. It would be more accurately called corporate socialism. This is the ubiquitous practice in which the costs of an enterprise are socialized—that is, they are borne by the public—while the profits remain private.

This is a model common to powerful businesses: they use their political influence to land windfalls for themselves at the taxpayers' expense. A good example may be your local sports stadium. Chances are it was built at the expense of the taxpayers; if so, its costs were socialized, while its profits remain private.

You own it, but you have to pay to use it. You paid for it, but don't look for a dividend check.

The leading business cronies of this model—entailing socialized costs for the people and private profits for the businesses—change as the economy changes. In the Gilded Age, the railroad companies were among the most powerful cronies of the State and were therefore favored with sweetheart treatment in all they did. In a free market, outsized profits attract the attention of other entrepreneurs whose entry into the market can be expected to unleash competition in services and rates—it is a check on the concentration of wealth and the growth of plutocracies. But State gifts of land and rights-of-way to the favored, its enforcement of route and transportation monopolies, government rate regulations, fare price fixing, strike repressions, and other anti-competitive measures protected the railroad cronies from competition and enriched them at the expense of the people.

American fruit companies operating in the banana republics of Central and South America were also among the leading cronies of the last century. They were so powerful that the Deep State, operating through figures like Allen Dulles, head of the CIA for eight and a half years beginning in 1953, and his brother John Foster Dulles, secretary of state for most of that period, arranged foreign assassinations and coups on their behalf.

Today, fruit companies and railroads are no longer dominant players among the Deep State's cronies. The mightiest arms of the Deep State today are the consortiums comprised of banks, Wall Street, and the Federal Reserve, along with digital-age giants like Google, and the national security-military-industrial complex.

The windfalls that State cronies receive breed a justified resentment among the people. People may not see the subsidies Boeing has gotten over the years from the Export-Import Bank—subsidies for Boeing's foreign aircraft buyers, subsidies that cannibalize America's economy as they enable those foreign airlines to compete more cheaply against US airlines. But it is hard to miss the bailouts the Federal Reserve and congress give to private banks. It is these bonanzas that build animosity. It is these jackpots that fuel the growth of the socialist movement in America.

Like the masses of Venezuela, the *Chavistas,* generations of Americans have been taught that they are entitled to live at the expense of others. They expect to be able to socialize their own cost of living. So conditioned, it is not a surprise that when confronted with State larceny like the bank bailouts, instead of opposing the plunder because theft is wrong, the entitled demand their own share of the spoils.

Entitlement expectations and resentment engendered by crony capitalism and the extreme wealth polarization that it produces have fueled movements like Occupy Wall Street and Antifa. A 2018 Gallup poll shows that a majority of Americans ages eighteen to twenty-nine approve of socialism over capitalism. The cronies have brought this state of affairs on themselves and will have themselves to blame if the future holds a "reign of terror" on wealth and the wealthy as the riots, arson, and plunder of 2020 so clearly threatened.

Allowing the Deep State's money manipulation to be thought a function of capitalism instead of crony capitalism explains the popularity of Alexandria Ocasio-Cortez, Elizabeth Warren, and Bernie Sanders. That they are right in a way about the power of the plutocracy does not excuse their economic confusion. One only need remember Sanders's announcement a few years ago that the American dream is more likely to be realized in banana republics like Venezuela than it is here. On the presidential campaign trail in 2016, when even the most ardent socialists could no longer deny the tragedy in Venezuela,

Sanders abruptly refused to talk about it. "I'm focused on my campaign," he dodged.

Raging Socialism

It hasn't taken socialist candidates and socialist parties to advance socialism in America. The Republicans and Democrats have done quite well on their own. Their success can be seen in the growth of government.

"It's a funny thing," said Milton Friedman, "after the fall of communism, everybody in the world agreed that socialism was a failure. Everybody in the world, more or less, agreed that capitalism was a success. And every capitalist country in the world apparently deduced from that, that what the West needed was more socialism."

In less than a century, entitlement spending has grown from less than 1 percent of GDP to nearly 17 percent today. Total government spending—federal, state, and local—was less the 7 percent of GDP in 1900. By 2000, after spikes in World War I and II, it had climbed to 30 percent. Today, total government spending is 38 percent of GDP.

All that spending is borne by the taxpayers; all government spending is by definition socialized spending. Its growth is unrelenting. In 1970, 12 percent of the population received Social Security benefits. Today, it's close to 20 percent, as sixty-four million Americans receive Social Security benefits; every day an additional eleven thousand Americans turn sixty-five. In 1945, there were forty-one workers for each beneficiary. Today, there are only 2.9. In ten years, that is expected to fall to only two full-time workers for each beneficiary.

The growing number of food stamp recipients and the rising cost of other social spending represents a huge growth in US socialism. The Deep State's Money Manipulators have played to the worst instincts of the elected classes. Like all socialists, the elected classes, whether of the left or right, are not disposed to care much for issues of cost. Today, they spend like banana republic dictators because the Federal Reserve has allowed Washington to borrow at rates so low that David Stockman described them as a mere "rounding errors."

"Washington thinks you can kick the can down the road, the debt is more or less free, and we'll get around to solving the problem. But today, let's not make any tough choices. That's where we are," says Stockman.

The issue of cost, of price, and of money, brings us back to the role that burgeoning socialism will play in *The Last Gold Rush...Ever*. While Paul Samuelson, whose economic textbooks indoctrinated generations of college students, proclaimed that "a socialist command economy can function and even thrive," it proved to be untrue. Almost a hundred years ago a wiser economist, Ludwig von Mises, explained exactly why socialism spells economic ruin for nations.

Mises demonstrated that because it lacked a price mechanism, socialism was utterly incapable of allocating resources and prioritizing economic activity efficiently. How can resources flow to where they are most essential and used most efficiently? How can competing demands be compared? How can advantageous substitute resources be discovered? Money calculation "provides a guide amid the bewildering throng of possibilities," said Mises. Without prices, "all production by lengthy and roundabout processes would be so many steps in the dark."

Without money calculation—and profit and loss—socialism can't calculate. Its failure is certain.

Mises' argument didn't stop demagogues nor dogmatic and political socialists, but serious academic socialists found his critique devastating. In their desperation to save socialism, they tried to find non-price substitutes for prices, contrivances like costly trial and error and the imputation of prices as proxies for actual prices. Soviet planners even resorted to using the prices in American Sears catalogs as proxies for prices to help them infer values. The result was confusion, waste, and poverty.

Socialist models have been ghastly failures everywhere: in the Soviet Union and Mao's China; in the failed African states of 1960s revolutionaries with names like Nkrumah, Nyerere, Kaunda; in North Korea and East Germany; in Albania and Cambodia; among all the Sandinistas and Fidelistas and all the other banana republic economic basket cases; and vividly played out before our eyes today in the tragedy of the Chavistas and Venezuela.

No more lab experiments are needed.

This is where we are: Politicians, loathe to consider the costs and consequence of their policies to begin with, are now operating in an environment in which prices no longer convey needed market information about supply and demand. Manipulated interest rates mislead businesses and misdirect resources since they don't reflect real conditions of capital availability and the real credit worthiness of borrowers. ("Are interest rates not prices? And if so, should they not be discovered instead of imposed?" —James Grant). The Fed has destroyed this price discovery function of the capital markets. The result is malinvestment. Into this mess of the blind leading the blind, factor in the new ascendency of explicit socialism and its unbroken run of failure.

Double-entry bookkeeping has been justly praised for its contribution to capitalism and the proliferation of prosperity. Goethe called it among the finest inventions of the human mind. Now, we have entered quite an opposite period, a new era in which the crucial function of price and fiscal reckoning of any responsible sort is neglected by lawmakers, undermined by monetary authorities, and is of no importance to the people.

Only economic chaos can result.

Someone once said that gold is capital on strike. Refusing to be victimized by the ruinous fruits of socialism, farsighted people move their wealth to gold. Socialism is another accelerant of *The Last Gold Rush…Ever.*

CHAPTER 7

THE EMPIRE'S END

The Harder They Fall

The first panacea for a mismanaged nation is inflation of the currency; the second is war. Both bring a temporary prosperity; both bring a permanent ruin. But both are the refuge of political and economic opportunists.

—Ernest Hemingway

The Rise...

It can't be known today whether the American Global Military Empire will end in a bang or with a whimper. Either way, an ignoble end of the Empire is the seventh and final reason to be prepared for *The Last Gold Rush...Ever*.

Americans are dangerously naïve about, and woefully ill-prepared for, the ending of their Global Military Empire. People who live in places like Greece and Italy are constantly surrounded by the grandeur of antiquity and the remnants of civilizations that came and went thousands of years ago. In the United States, antiquities date back a couple of hundred years.

It's worse in the western US, where a building that is not even a hundred years old can be an object of historical preservation.

With such a short historical horizon, Americans think the government will always be the government. They think the money will always be the money.

But everybody in Europe and most of the rest of the world knows that the government won't always be the government and the money won't always be the money. In their national memories and visible daily in the monuments that surround them, they have the remnants of governments that were here today and gone tomorrow, monetary systems that crashed almost as soon as they were contrived. They've seen the evidence of dukes and princes and monarchs who passed by one after another. They've watched a parade of elected leaders with imperial ambitions come and go.

Consider all the empires that came to an end in the last century: the Austrian-Hungarian and the Ottoman empires; those of Nazi Germany and Imperial Japan; the British, French, and Netherlands' empires; and the evil empire of the Soviet Union.

Over and over, the rest of the world has experienced what Americans have not: military expansionism, nation-building, and the military domination of foreign populations, accompanied by State spending that led to bankruptcy and monetary failure.

The United States spent the twentieth century becoming an empire. It first succumbed to the imperial impulse with the Spanish-American War, putting its footprints in places from the Caribbean and Central America to the Philippines. It was a blatant beginning, but modest nonetheless compared to the unstoppable momentum of global interventionism that would follow.

In what many thought were America's halcyon days after World War II, the growth and maintenance of the Global Military Empire went mostly unquestioned. With victory in World War II, the Empire's troops were left behind in Germany and Japan as the decades rolled by (just as they would later remain in Korea), in numbers sufficient only for any outbreak of hostilities to serve as a tripwire, ensuring Americans would fight any new war in the region no matter whether their interests were truly at stake.

At the same time, the US gave Cold War security guarantees to countries that could only draw the nation into conflagrations in far-flung places that are of no material interest to the defense of the American people.

As Pat Buchanan critically observed in the heat of the Iraq war, in his book *Day of Reckoning*: "Between the alliance with France in the Revolutionary War in 1778 and the creation of NATO in 1949, the United States did not enter a formal alliance with any country. Yet we are now treaty-bound to defend 60 nations on five continents."

As the American Empire spread, it went to and fro upon the face of the earth, arming and bribing a succession of murderous dictators, assassinating officials, and secretly toppling foreign governments. In the 1950s, it covertly sowed the wind in far flung places like Iran and Guatemala.

By the 1960s, the growth of the Empire and a confrontation with its unsettling realities was shattering illusions of innocence about the US nation-state. Among the imperial initiatives of the decade was the CIA's 1961 invasion of Cuba at the Bay of Pigs. That fiasco resulted in the 1962 Cuban missile crisis that brought the world to the doorstep of a nuclear holocaust. By any account—from the official conclusion of the Warren Commission to the latest findings based on more than fifty years of subsequent discoveries and troves of declassified and other documents—the assassination of President Kennedy that followed the next year was causally linked to the Empire's Cuban activities.

With the collapse of the Soviet Union, the business of the American Global Military Empire became the full-throttle obsession of US policy makers, one now made explicit in new policy doctrines full of vainglory and ambition. The military-industrial complex of which President Eisenhower warned ("This conjunction of an immense military establishment and a large arms industry is new in the American experience…. We must not fail to comprehend its grave implications"), the beneficiary of trillions of dollars spent during the Cold War, moved quickly to stake a fresh, new claim to the people's wealth before a "peace dividend" could be declared with the end of the Cold War.

The new policies and think-tank products were replete with talk of unilateralism, the US as guarantor of a new world order, and preemptive military actions. Deep thinkers celebrated the period as "the Unipolar Moment" and even "the End of History." Full of these new doctrines and age-old hubris, politicians soon put armies in Saudi Arabia, expanded NATO to the doorstep of Russia, and pivoted to Asia, believing righteously that the rest of mankind would bend readily to the will of the US imperial state.

But as the imperious Pentagon Goliath was talking about "full-spectrum dominance," the Davids were piling up smooth stones—and box-cutters. Even the fact that it reaped whirl-winds from its prior interventionism has not been enough to stop the State from continuing to play its dangerous game of dominance in places like Iraq, Afghanistan, Libya, Syria, and Ukraine, visiting economic collapse and civil war on each as it went.

Despite the vanity of its presumptions, attitudes beyond our shores about the US were changing. Indeed, Americans were thunderstruck when the new century was accompanied by the discovery that the Atlantic and Pacific oceans no longer insulated them from blowback, the angry repercussions for its military meddling and covert operations hither and yon. Waiting in the wings with its own ferocious impact is the other reality, that keeping the activities of the State—expansionist at home as well as abroad—financed, has meant low or no economic growth, massive monetary manipulation, and a national debt that depends on foreign creditors.

In their slumber, the majority of the American people have missed the growth of the Empire, its accompanying rise of authoritarianism, and the recklessness with which it is squandering their prosperity. For those more vigilant it is apparent the US reached an inflection point with the blunder of the elective war in Iraq. President Reagan's national security director, General William Odom, rightly called it "the greatest strategic disaster in United States history."

Now, the unsustainable American Global Military Empire has begun to show its overextension. Just as the costs of the Vietnam war were instrumental in the collapse of the post-World War II Bretton Woods gold exchange monetary system and responsible for the painful stagflation of the 1970s, it is no coincidence that hard on the heels of George W. Bush's war on Iraq, the American economy entered into the Great Recession, the worst economic downturn since the Great Depression.

As the interventionist State lurched into the twenty-first century, this hard economic reality played out against a background of perpetual war and made it inevitable that more Americans—except perhaps in Washington—would awaken to what Chalmers Johnson called "the sorrows of empire." The age-old way of Empire meant the State was becoming ever more authoritarian and secretive as it engaged in clandestine and illegal operations, not only abroad, but within its own borders. While these activities of the State were increasingly cloaked in black budgets, brazen lies, and secrecy, the private affairs of the people were expected to become a wide-open book to the State, the Fourth Amendment notwithstanding.

Mark Twain was right. America cannot have an empire abroad and a republic at home.

Sizing Up the Empire

Today, the United States is responsible for about a third of the world's total military spending. Its warfare outlays exceed those of the next nine countries combined. On any given day there are ten thousand US Special Forces operating in secret somewhere among two-thirds of the world's countries.

The US may be $27 trillion in debt, but cost has been no object to the Defense Department. It has spread US bases far and wide across the face of the earth. In 2019, David Vine, author of *Base Nation: How US Military Bases Abroad Harm America and the World*, and his colleagues reported that seventy-five years after World War II ended, there remain 194 US base sites in Germany and 121 in Japan. In South Korea, more than two generations after the war, there are 83 US bases. Hundreds of thousands of American military personnel are deployed on 800 US military installations in more than seventy countries around the world.

"Rarely does anyone consider how we would feel with a foreign base on US soil, or how we would react if Russia, China, or Iran built even a single base near our borders today," writes Vine. "For most in the United States, the idea of even the nicest, most benign foreign troops arriving with their tanks, planes, and high-powered weaponry and making themselves at home in our country—occupying and fencing off hundreds or thousands of acres of our land—is unthinkable."

Vine points out that Russia has only nine bases in former Soviet republics. "In total all the non-US countries of the world have about thirty foreign bases among them—as compared to the United States and its eight hundred or so."

A few more reference points reveal the dimensions of the Empire:

- As overt US operations moved into Syria in the initiative against ISIS, military affairs analyst and historian Andrew Bacevich put the number of countries in the Greater Middle East in which Americans have killed or been killed, countries the US has invaded, occupied or bombed at fourteen—*just since 1980*:

- "Let's tick them off: Iran (1980, 1987–1988); Libya (1981, 1986, 1989, 2011); Lebanon (1983); Kuwait (1991); Iraq (1991–2011, 2014–); Somalia

(1992–1993, 2007–); Bosnia (1995); Saudi Arabia (1991, 1996); Afghanistan (1998, 2001–); Sudan (1998); Kosovo (1999); Yemen (2000, 2002–); Pakistan (2004–); and now Syria."

- The former US ambassador to Saudi Arabia Charles W. Freeman Jr. offered this perspective in 2016: "The United States has now been engaged in a cold war with Iran—Persia—for thirty-seven years. It has conducted various levels of hot war in Iraq for twenty-six years. It has been in combat in Afghanistan for fifteen years. Americans have bombed Somalia for fifteen, Libya for five, and Syria for one and a half years. One war has led to another. None has yielded any positive result and none shows any sign of doing so."

- To complete the picture, consider that there are fewer than 200 countries in the entire world. During fiscal year 2014, the US deployed special operations forces in 133 countries.

- Vine and his colleagues maintain that this global presence has "fueled a hyper-interventionist foreign policy by making war look like an easy solution. Since 1980, U.S. administrations have used bases at least 23 times to launch military interventions…"

An empire on such a growth path will consume more and more resources until it finally consumes itself—like the snake swallowing its own tail. In the meantime, the demands of the war party in Washington continually become more assertive and more lawless.

The Empire's tangled web has seen Americans in Iraq fighting against their own weapons. While it warred with al-Qaeda and ISIS in Iraq, America bankrolled and armed those same groups in Libya. Jihadists in Syria, supported by the CIA, battled with fundamentalist militias armed by the Pentagon.

A consequence of the American Empire's wobbling concentration of power is that it reads its relative decline as a challenge demanding a military solution. It reacts militarily to its decline. In so doing, it traps itself in a bankrupting vicious cycle. In *The Rise and Fall of the Great Powers*, historian Paul Kennedy says, "Great powers in relative decline instinctively respond by spending more on 'security,' and thereby divert potential resources from 'investment' and compound their long-term dilemma."

The converse of the bankrupting cycle can also be true: nations that avoid the destruction of war can find their relative positions improved. While the US has pursued its foreign entanglements and elective wars in the Middle East and squandered the American people's patrimony on projects of empire, China has avoided entanglements and conserved its resources. It has grown and grabbed markets while the US pretended to manage the affairs of the globe. What could be more ironic than that after Saddam Hussein was toppled at the cost of American blood and treasure, the first major oil deal Iraq signed was with China?

Same as the Old Boss?

Americans have become fatigued by their wars and confused about their purposes. Many rejected Hillary Clinton's bid to become president specifically because of her warmongering ways. For others, Donald Trump's appeal was his promise to put an end to perpetual war. He insisted that Americans had been deceived into Iraq, that he was going to end its foreign wars and use American resources to make America great again. But as he surrounded himself with hawks and arms industry executives, it became evident early on that the Deep State would continue to call the shots, just as it remained in charge when Barack Obama promised to end the wars in Iraq and Afghanistan. The new administration had only been in place for two months when a March 23, 2017, *US News & World Report* opinion piece headlined "Trump's Wars" captured the reality economically: "The president is doubling down on the Middle East quagmires he once criticized."

In the last year of Trump's term, military budgets have grown ceaselessly (with an emphasis on offensive, not defensive weapons.) Trump's 2019 budget called for $716 billion in Pentagon spending. That was an $82 billion leap from the year before. "I've given you the biggest budget in our history, and I've now done it two times…" said Trump at the Pentagon in early 2019, "and I am about to do it three times." And indeed, the 2020 military budget swelled to $738 billion.

War-weary Americans have a hard time pointing to anywhere that the Deep State's elective interventionism has been reversed under Trump. Here's a brief survey of engagements and targets:

- A mantra of the Reagan administration claimed that "personnel is policy." Trump surrounded himself with some of the most bellicose officials possible, most visibly John Bolton, who served as national security advisor in 2018 and 2019, and secretary of state Mike

Pompeo. Bolton, who long called for attacking North Korea, is widely believed to have been responsible for torpedoing the 2019 Hanoi summit between Trump and Kim Jong-un. It remains to be seen if North Korea can be denuclearized and if the Korean War can finally be brought to an end. But it was certainly not lost on Kim Jong-un that both Bolton and vice president Mike Pence have threatened North Korea with "the Libya model." Colonel Muammar Gaddafi agreed to give up Libya's weapons of mass destruction and allow international weapons inspections, only to be toppled and killed a few years later when his only possible deterrence was gone. ("We decimated that country," said Trump.)

- In December 2018, when the president said we were leaving Syria "now," both Bolton and Pompeo fell all over themselves to explain that it didn't mean the US was actually "leaving."

- For years, private citizen Donald Trump called for the US to come home from Afghanistan. A 2013 Twitter message was typical: "We should leave Afghanistan immediately. No more wasted lives." Perhaps a portion of the troops will be brought home, but the *New York Times* reported in February 2019 that Pentagon plans called for a withdrawal to take place over three to five years. From past experience it is easy to conclude that that means an indefinite stay, as one draw-down plan after another has failed in America's longest war, often resulting in an increase in troops instead. In any case, remaining troops in both Syria and Afghanistan are enough to serve as a tripwire to assure future US involvement.

- Trump has insisted the US would not continue acting as the world's policeman, yet he remained committed to supporting the Saudi slaughter in Yemen and vetoed a congressional measure to reign in its unauthorized war collaboration there.

- Although having been critical of US regime change wars, Trump appears to have wanted his own in broken-down Venezuela. "That's the country we should be going to war with," Trump said, according to one account. "They have all that oil and they're right on our back door." Multiple accounts since 2017 have reported him asking about the possibility of invading Venezuela.

- If NATO has outlived its usefulness, as candidate Trump insisted on the campaign trail, then why has Trump suggested bringing Brazil into the "obsolete" organization?

- Trump promised to warm relations with Russia, but his serial sanctions on Russia and NATO's push eastward have delivered Cold War II. Putin, responding to what he sees as an American policy of encirclement, has been candid about major developments in Russia's weapons arsenal, most notably nuclear-powered cruise missiles and sophisticated new means of evading missile defense systems. In that environment, Trump announced the US would pull out of President Reagan's INF

(Intermediate-Range Nuclear Forces) Treaty; Russia withdrew from the pact in response.

- On close inspection there is something almost surrealistic in US policy toward Russia in this and in prior administrations. President Trump's National Security Strategy published in December 2017 charges Russia with "threatening behavior, such as nuclear posturing and the forward deployment of offensive capabilities."

- Yet the same document is full of talk of forward deployment and threatening nuclear posturing of its own: "...the assurance capabilities provided by our nuclear Triad and by U.S. theater nuclear capabilities deployed abroad"; "[f]ear of escalation will not prevent the United States from defending our vital interests and those of our allies and partners."

- We described in chapter 5 the Warsaw summit organized by the US in 2019 for what Israeli prime minister Netanyahu said was "to advance the common interest of war with Iran." Shortly thereafter, at Netanyahu's urging, Trump designated Iran's Revolutionary Guard a terrorist organization. This is akin to a declaration of war during the open-ended US war on terror, but this time, and for the first time, it is directed at a part of a foreign government. While Bolton had long signaled his support for Iranian regime change, Pompeo also sought Pentagon plans to launch "retaliatory strikes" against Iran. Clearly Pompeo is among those who led the charge for the killing of Iranian Major General Qassim Soleimani, an official of a country with which the US is not at war, in a strike that took place in a third country, Iraq, which had not agreed to an attack. The event is complicated by reports that Soleimani was in Iraq as a peace emissary, mediating tensions between Saudi Arabia and Iran.

- Although Trump has questioned US war guarantees given away promiscuously in the postwar era—the US has twenty-eight war guarantees in Europe alone—Pompeo nevertheless affirmed a US defense commitment to the Philippines and its erratic president, Rodrigo Duterte. Only a month later, Duterte was threatening China with a Philippine "suicide mission" over claims in the South China Sea.

While the prospect of US interventions and wars in places like Venezuela and Iran are substantial, the most dangerous probability is a war with China arising from claims and incidents in the South China Sea. The number of maritime confrontations is rising; the chances of an incident that escalates grows more real daily. The economic consequences and the impact of a confrontation with China for both the dollar and gold are important enough to demand a closer look at the presuppositions that can ensure a needless tragedy.

Deconstructing a Deep State Talking Point

Despite a decision by the voters for a change of course, it should be clear that the Trump administration has represented for the most part a continuum of the Deep State's foreign policy. It is what Glenn Greenwald (who published reports detailing Edward Snowden's revelations) calls the "core premise of America's foreign policy—that it has the right to bomb any country in the world."

It was clear from the early days of the Trump administration that US foreign policy would remain largely unchanged in the South China Sea. Confirmation could be found in a May 2017 *Wall Street Journal* story. If the Obama "pivot" to Asia meant the South China Sea would be treated as though it were an American lake, it was steady as she goes in the new Trump administration: "WASHINGTON—The Pentagon conducted a Navy patrol in the South China Sea, US officials said Wednesday, the first such operation under President Donald Trump designed to send a signal to China about US intentions to keep critical sea lanes open in the Pacific Ocean."

The initiated will recognize this as a core premise of the Deep State's consensus foreign policy, that the US Empire is required "to keep the sea lanes open." It is beyond the scope of this book to rebut the totality of the Deep State's positions, those that become the bipartisan and unquestioned polices of the US government. But this front of the American Empire provides as clear lessons as any that even in the presence of sensible and proven non-interventionist alternatives, the default position of the Deep State is always in favor of interventionism that piles up debt for the people and enriches the military-industrial complex.

The sea lanes talking point reached a fevered pitch with the Obama "pivot" policy that called for an increased US military presence in Southeast Asia and the Pacific. Trump's campaign-trail displays of antagonism toward China, coupled with his across-the-board escalation of military spending, including a commitment to a colossal increase in America's naval fleet, focuses our attention on this specific Deep State policy.

Who exactly is it that has been threatening the sea lanes? China?

China's interest is in keeping the sea lanes open, as it is utterly dependent on the importation of oil and its shipment through both the faraway Strait of Hormuz and closer by, through the Malacca Strait. As China has grown economically over the last several decades, it is simply unavoidable that its presence in the region's waterways would grow. It cannot be otherwise. In fact, some 75 percent of all commercial shipping through the South China Sea is coming from or going to China.

If China itself were to try to close lanes in the South China Sea to other countries, like the US and Japan, its own economy—vying to be the largest in the world—would collapse with the departure of its largest customers. Millions of suddenly unemployed Chinese workers would pose an existential threat to the central government. And that—an internal upheaval—is what keeps the autocrats in Beijing awake at night.

If the US can be justified in patrolling oceans close to China halfway around the world to protect its own commercial lifelines, cannot China be justified in doing the same in the waterways of its own neighborhood?

Indeed, it is the US naval chokehold on shipping in its near seas that keeps China alarmed. It is well aware of the precedent of the US embargo on oil shipments and the closing off of the Panama Canal to Japan before World War II.

Is there today any justification for China's alarm? "We will remain the principal security power in the Asia-Pacific for decades to come," vowed Obama's secretary of defense Ashton Carter. He then spelled out US plans for the Asia-Pacific region:

> [N]ot only increasing the number of US military personnel in the region, part of some 365,000 assigned to the Asia-Pacific today, but also sending and stationing some of our most advanced capabilities there.
>
> That includes F-22 and F-35 stealth fighter jets, P-8 Poseidon maritime surveillance aircraft, continuous deployments of B-2 and B-52 strategic bombers, and also our newest surface warfare ships like the amphibious assault ship USS *America* and all three of our newest class of stealth destroyers, the DDG-1000, which will be all home-ported with the Pacific Fleet. And all the while we're bringing America's regional force posture into the twenty-first century by rotating American personnel into new and more places like northern Australia and new sites in the Philippines and modernizing our existing footprint in Japan and the Republic of Korea.

He may represent a different president of a different party, one who promised a different foreign policy, but there is no daylight to be found between Carter's pledge to remain dominant in the region "for decades to come," and secretary of state Mike Pompeo's insistence that China's activities are a threat to the security and livelihood of the US. Carter's plans and Pompeo's pronouncements demonstrate that the US intends to remain a formidable military presence in a region that is a tangled spaghetti plate of conflicting and overlapping territorial claims and Air Defense Identification Zones. China, Brunei, Malaysia, the Philippines, Taiwan, and Vietnam all voice claims in the South China Sea. Similarly, China, Japan, and the Republic of China (Taiwan) all make claims to the Senkaku (Diaoyu) Islands in the East China Sea. Further, India is becoming more assertive in advancing its claims in the Indian Ocean.

The Deep State is pivoting to a region already ripe with the risk of miscalculation. While competing maritime claims are an inevitable source of conflict, the US is simply not capable of solving this plethora of claims, ancient and recent, involving territorial rights, shipping lanes, and artificial islands, any more than it can actually keep the sea lanes open.

All it can do is add to the proliferation of military hardware in the region.

It is past time to ask why it is the responsibility of the US to be the military arbiter of such claims. It rings hollow to answer, as the US does, that it takes no position on competing territorial claims in the South China Sea. In his humorous "Extracts from Adam's Diary," Mark Twain describes Eve wondering why the lions and tigers in the Garden of Eden, armed with such fearsome claws and teeth, subsist on flowers and grass when they are more suitably equipped for killing and eating each other. If the Empire takes no position on competing territorial claims in the region, why does it need to concentrate so much military might there?

The US pretense is not convincing to anyone in the region. The US offered the same hollow disclaimer to Saddam Hussein before he invaded Kuwait, that the US took no position on Arab-Arab conflicts, such as Iraq's border disagreement with Kuwait.

As it turned out, the US took a very substantial position on the border dispute it had disclaimed.

The Empire's alliance politics in the South China Sea region are aimed like a laser beam at China. In a May 2016 visit to Hanoi, President Obama ended an arms embargo on Vietnam. Because of the Empire's addiction to power politics around the world (with the ever-present encouragement of the weapons manufacturers of the military-industrial complex), the US will now arm the Vietnamese government with which it warred not so many years ago at the cost of more than fifty-eight thousand American lives.

Would there be an outcry in the US if China were to agree to begin selling lethal weapons to Mexico? But that analogy is inexact since US war spending is three or four times that of China. It would be more accurate to ask how the US would react if a superpower of hegemonic appetites and with proportionately greater military means were to begin selling lethal weapons to Mexico, while eyeing Mexican ports as a base for its warships to patrol the coast of California as a check on US activities, much as the US has its sights on eventual naval operations from Vietnam's deepwater port of Cam Ranh Bay.

Such analogies don't carry much weight with the Empire's committed global hegemonists. Theirs is a "might makes right" outlook, that as long as what they perceive to be a unipolar moment remains, they will insist that the world bow to the will of the US. That engenders the resentment of the US discussed earlier.

In challenging the global interventionist presupposition, it must be asked if keeping sea lanes open is worth the cost of war, especially in the nuclear age. There are precedents that allow us to answer the question.

What was called the 1973 Arab oil embargo (although not all Arab countries participated) provides a place to begin. First Libya, quickly followed by Saudi Arabia and other Arab oil producing states, placed an embargo on all oil shipments to the US. In Europe the embargo was extended to the Netherlands; the UK and France were not targeted.

Although shipping lanes to the US and other targets were not closed, the effect was the same.

The embargo lasted from October 1973 to March 1974. In the public imagination, the embargo had the effect of starving the US of vital energy supplies. But what actually happened to oil imports?

They continued to rise.

Energy journalist and author Robert Bryce (*Gusher of Lies: The Dangerous Delusions of "Energy Independence"*) writes that "America's crude oil imports in 1973 exceeded 1972 levels by 372 million barrels. In 1974, imports jumped again, exceeding 1973 level by 85 million barrels." It was the rising prices and gas lines at the time that created the impression in the minds of Americans that they had suffered a crippling supply interruption. But rising prices were the inevitable result of Nixon's suspension of US dollar convertibility to gold in 1971.

Foreign oil producers wondered why they should sell their appreciating oil, brought forth from the depths of the earth at real expense, for depreciating dollars created without limitation by nothing more than bookkeeping entries. OPEC had repeatedly warned that a fall in the dollar's purchasing power would result in higher nominal oil prices. The shortages and gas lines were the result of State interference in the market with labyrinthine pricing and byzantine refining regulations that grew out of Richard Nixon's eerily Soviet-sounding 1971 "New Economic Policy" and its multiple phases of convoluted interventions. As Bryce notes, because of shortages, a thousand gas stations *had already closed months before the embargo began.*

As would be expected with the closing of sea lanes, Washington's war response to the embargo kicked in right away. Secretary of state Henry Kissinger muttered darkly about "countermeasures" and wrote years later in his memoirs that "these were not empty threats." It wasn't until the release of a British intelligence file on the affair in 2004 that we learned just what was under consideration: the invasion of Saudi Arabia, Kuwait, and Bahrain.

The British report was the direct result of bellicose remarks by defense secretary James Schlesinger to the British ambassador. He recorded that Schlesinger commented in the inartful language of war threats that "it was no longer obvious to him that the United States could not use force."

The conversation was of enough concern to British prime minister Edward Heath that he ordered an inquiry into US intentions. The British intelligence report found that US seizure of oil fields, "the possibility uppermost in American thinking," would consist of an initial operation in "the order of two brigades, one for Saudi operation, one for Kuwait and possibly a third for Abu Dhabi."

The Arab oil embargo quickly proved its ineffectiveness and was over in less than six months, far shorter than the ten years following an invasion that British intelligence estimated an American occupation would have to last.

Like water that flows downhill, oil flows to those that pay for it. If it encounters an obstacle in one channel, it finds another. If one buyer is being embargoed, or one sea lane is closed, it will flow in a different way. The examples in international trade are legion. During the Iran-Iraq War, Iraq built pipelines, including a trans-Saudi pipeline to the Red Sea, to avoid the Iranian adjacency to the strategic Strait of Hormuz. Saudi Arabia and the United Arab Emirates have recently added pipelines to bypass Hormuz as well.

During the immediacy of the 1973 embargo, it soon became obvious that Arab state oil not sold to the US was sold to other buyers, reducing the amount of oil those buyers would purchase from producers not involved in the embargo. That freed up their production to be redirected to the US and other embargoed nations. The Arab oil producers could stop direct sales to the United States but had no control over the secondary markets of the world.

To the extent Arab oil production was reduced, it was offset by higher production elsewhere. The Arab producers could have stopped pumping oil altogether. That would have had an impact, but one felt primarily on their own balance sheets, and that was not what they had in mind. They had oil and they needed to sell it. As Saddam Hussein asked before the Gulf War, "What do they think we're going to do with the oil? Drink it?"

In trying to rally the American people's support for that war, secretary of state James Baker explained the war was about "jobs, jobs, jobs." It was a startlingly candid admission, one that should have provoked a double take on the part of thoughtful people. The Deep State was urging another war that would send Americans and blameless people elsewhere to their death, for the sake of the US employment rate. As callous as was Baker's admission, it was even worse economics. The unemployment rate *rose for sixteen months after the war for jobs was over*, topping out at 1.5 percent higher than when Baker spoke.

With the encouragement of an eager military-industrial complex, the American people have shouldered security costs for Europeans and for Japan, each far more dependent on foreign oil than is the US. Yet those beneficiaries have been more pragmatic and more frugal. In his prescient 2000 book *Blowback: The Cost and Consequences of American Empire*, Chalmers Johnson described the extraordinary US military expenditures in the Persian Gulf region—even before they spiked after 9/11—writing that it was responsible for about $50 billion of the annual US defense budget, "including maintenance of one or more carrier task forces there, protecting sea lanes, and keeping large air forces in readiness in the area. But the oil we import costs only a fifth that amount, about $11 billion per annum. Middle Eastern oil accounts for 10 percent of US consumption, 25 percent of Europe's, and half of that of Japan, which contributes in inverse proportion to maintaining a G-7 military presence there. It is not that Europe and Japan are incapable of securing their own oil supplies through commercial treaties, diplomacy, or military activity, but that America's global hegemony makes it unnecessary for them to do so."

In other words, the American people were being taxed about $5 of protection costs for every $1.10 they spent on actual Persian Gulf petroleum.

Formulated as they were before 9/11, Johnson's numbers are today woefully low. After a detailed analysis, Princeton University economic geographer Roger Stern estimates the cost of the US military presence in the Persian Gulf from 1976 to 2010 at a breathtaking and bank-breaking $8 trillion.

That's nearly a third of the current US national debt.

Exactly why should the shipping industry, foreign and domestic alike, be allowed to socialize its costs of security instead of passing them along like any other expense to willing customers? It is even more egregious that foreign nations are allowed to socialize among US taxpayers the cost of securing their commerce. Similarly, the operators of foreign ports, for example those of the Gulf's oil-exporting nations, should be expected to keep their own nearby waterways and transit zones safe by means of "commercial treaties, diplomacy, or military activity" at their own expense, or else find their customers have deserted them.

If Americans have been made the milk cows of European and Japanese oil users, paying for benefits that other nations don't find valuable enough to pay for themselves, they have no one to blame but their own government.

One more observation can help lay the Empire's sea lane rationale to rest. At the beginning of the 1967 Six-Day War, Egypt closed one of the world's most important sea lanes, the Suez Canal. It remained closed for eight years. Since the Suez Canal is the most direct route from Europe to Asia, today carrying about 7.5 percent of all seagoing commerce, important conclusions can be drawn from its long closure.

By analyzing major factors like average increases in shipping distances between countries caused by the canal closure and any resulting reduction in trade, and by estimating the contribution of seaborne commerce to GDP, one can come up with a rough estimate of the consequent overall reduction in GDP. John Quiggin, an economist at the University of Queensland, has estimated the cost of the Suez closure for the UK at six-tenths of 1 percent of GDP; for France it was about three-tenths of 1 percent of GDP.

Because economics involves comparisons and trade-offs, the next step would be to compare those unfortunate but modest costs to GDP with the ever-escalating cost of warfare.

NATO urges its members to commit 2 percent of GDP to warfare spending. The UK has been a little over, France a little under that target. (The US spends over 3.6 percent and shoulders about 75 percent of the NATO budget.) So the rough impact of the Suez closure turns out to be only a small fraction, less than a third of the UK's and about 15 percent of France's military spending. Since military spending rises substantially in wartime, it is clear that the cost of dislocated shipping is even less than the military budgets that would prevail in war. For the US, affected much less than Europe by the Suez closing and spending more of its GDP on war, the impact as a fraction of its military spending is much smaller still.

Quiggin applies the principle to the South China Sea shipping routes, observing, as we have, that the majority of the trade there is coming from or going to China. "The remaining $1 trillion or so of trade (about 1.5 percent of global GDP) might, in the event of a crisis, be forced to take more circuitous routes, as happened when the Suez Canal was blocked. But using the same method as was applied to Suez, it's easy to see that the total impact would be modest."

The nature of empires justifies Quiggin's skepticism that any type of cost-benefit analysis will matter much in policy decisions. Often things that matter even more than financial costs are weighed still less. It is shocking to confront just how little human lives account for in these machinations.

Those suffering illusions about the Deep State's willingness to consign people to death in its war pretexts should recall the words of Henry Kissinger, the modern era's secretary of state most celebrated by the lapdog press. In *The Final Days*, their account of the end of the Nixon administration, Bob Woodward and Carl Bernstein write that "Kissinger referred pointedly to military men as 'dumb, stupid animals to be used' as pawns for foreign policy."

Imperial Overstretch

The project of empire has been an expensive undertaking for the US. And yet Republicans and Democrats are both willing to see it continue. Both are willing to extend American war guarantees to additional countries and to increase military spending. But just as the cost of the Vietnam War made it impossible for the US to keep its "good as gold" dollar promise, the costs of the post-9/11 empire will break what remains of the dollar's reputation.

Still, no record of serial failures is ever long enough to dissuade the interventionists and warmongers from their schemes.

Because of the Roman Empire's scope and endurance, it is often taken as the archetype for the fate of empires. Edward Gibbon's venerable *The History of the Decline and Fall of the Roman Empire* set a standard for later studies. It is a monumental work of six volumes, the first of which was published the year the Declaration of Independence was signed. Gibbons might today say simply that Rome collapsed under the weight of its "multitasking."

He wrote, "The decline of Rome was the natural and inevitable effect of immoderate greatness. Prosperity ripened the principle of decay; the cause of the destruction multiplied with the extent of conquest; and, as soon as time or accident had removed the artificial supports, the stupendous fabric yielded to the pressure of its own weight. The story of the ruin is simple and obvious: and instead of inquiring why the Roman Empire was destroyed we should rather be surprised that it has subsisted for so long."

Gibbon's conclusions can be supplemented by a modern survey of the great Western powers over the last five hundred years. In arguing that an empire's domestic economy suffers underinvestment as resources are diverted to foreign entanglements, historian Paul Kennedy gets to the very heart of the self-limiting nature of empires. He writes that "a top-heavy military establishment may slow down the rate of economic growth and lead to a decline in the nation's share of world manufacturing output and therefore wealth, and therefore power."

Power does not arrive on the national scene full-born and bearing arms like Athena erupting from the head of Zeus. Wealth is its precondition; production precedes wealth. In the face of the relative decline of its manufacturing dominance, the US now finds itself in what Kennedy calls "imperial overstretch," a position that historians of empires have seen again and again. Kennedy writes, "The sum total of the United States' global interests and obligations is nowadays far larger than the country's power to defend them all simultaneously."

The State has no real understanding of prosperity. The State creates no wealth. The only wealth it has it gets by taking it from those who do create wealth. But the State does understand command and war. As the expression has it, "When you're holding a hammer, everything looks like a nail." And so, the Empire reacts militarily to its inarguable relative decline.

America has forgotten the lessons of what has been called the "American Century" when, as Pat Buchanan observes in *A Republic, Not an Empire*, America emerged from the chaos and destruction of each of the world wars as an unrivalled productive powerhouse, because it managed to keep much of its economic powder dry:

> In World War I Americans did not go into combat in great numbers until 1918. In World War II America did not cross the Channel until four years after France had fallen, and three years after the USSR had begun fighting for its life. We did not go to war against Japan until the Japanese army had been bogged down for four years fighting a no-win war against the most populous nation on earth. US casualties in the two world wars were thus the smallest of the Great Powers, and America in the twentieth century has never known the vast destruction that was visited on Russia, Germany, and Japan—on even on France and England.

Historian A. J. P. Taylor made the point this way: "Though the object of being a Great Power is to be able to fight a Great War, the only way of remaining a Great Power is not to fight one."

The Bigger They Come, The Harder They Fall

While the dynamics that drive the creation of empires are many and may occur in combination with one another—pillage and plunder, religion, race, subjugation and enslavement, ambitious and energetic leadership, ideology, the exploitation of new discoveries, resource imperialism—there is one factor universal in their decline: empires unwind when they are no longer affordable.

Quite plainly, some nations can no longer afford their empires for the simple fact that they have been conquered in war. Among the empires that ended in the last century were those of Germany and Japan, both crushed in World War II.

The only thing faster than Germany's rise from the ashes of defeat after World War I, as it transformed itself into the world's second largest industrial economy, was its subsequent collapse. The Third Reich was to have been a Thousand Year Reich. (The word *Reich* can mean realm, state, or even kingdom. But it is etymologically related to the English word *reach* and can be literally translated into *empire*.)

For Adolf Hitler, the future of Germany was simple: *Weltmacht Oder Niedergang*, world domination or ruin. Imperial domination meant a mad spree of military spending, which in 1938 had grown to 4,500 percent that of 1930.

In the end, the Reich, warring to the east and the west, was ruined by the overreach of its empire. In the last days of the war, the army was increasingly comprised of children as even thirteen-year-old boys were pressed into service.

Imperial Japan had taken Taiwan from China, annexed Korea, and invaded Manchuria before Pearl Harbor. After Pearl Harbor, it grabbed Singapore, Indonesia, Malay, Thailand, and parts of Burma, China, and the Philippines.

But even before Pearl Harbor, Japan had become a state-planned economy, with bureaucrats establishing production quotas and setting profits. It was already undergoing rationing of food, clothing, and many other goods. By 1938, warfare accounted for 70 percent of government spending.

Japan's fate was implicit in Hitler's misbegotten tenet of domination or ruin. In both nations, foreign domination led to ruin.

But empires don't just end for losers. They end for victors as well.

The world-straddling British Empire peaked after World War I and immediately began to shrink. At the time, interest on its national debt consumed almost 40 percent of government spending. Inflation doubled and the pound sterling collapsed.

The sun finally set on the British Empire after World War II. Over the following twenty years, the Empire's hold on people beyond its own shores fell from seven hundred million to five million.

Victory in two world wars left the British Empire, once the greatest since Rome, broke.

Empires and militarism are inseparable. Their expansionism is effectuated by force. They must be maintained by force. When force flags, when the treasury runs dry, the empire frays.

The Soviet Union was among the victors in World War II and became an empire thanks to the land grab granted Stalin by Roosevelt and Churchill in the war's waning days. To Russia's west, the Soviet Empire was allowed to gobble up East Germany, Poland, Czechoslovakia, Hungary, Romania, Bulgaria, Yugoslavia, and Albania. The powerless members of the Soviet's "Union" included the Baltic states: Latvia, Lithuania, and Estonia, seized in World War II, as well as Armenia, Azerbaijan, Belarus, Georgia, Kazakhstan, Kyrgyzstan, Moldova, Tajikistan, Turkmenistan, Ukraine, and Uzbekistan.

One of the visible triggers that helped bring the "Evil Empire" crashing down was the 1986 collapse in oil prices. Since the Soviet Union made almost nothing that the rest of the world wanted, it was utterly dependent on revenue from the energy sector. The Kremlin was faced with a "guns or butter" choice: make up the sudden shortfall in oil revenue by cutting the empire's military spending or starve even more the consumer economy—a shortage economy for almost seventy years to begin with. Instead, it decided to try to borrow its way out of the difficulty. By the time of the empire's crack-up, the Soviet's external debt had ballooned. Their empire had become unaffordable.

Like the British Empire, the fact that the Soviet Union hadn't been defeated in war wasn't enough to assure its survival. As Gibbon might have said, the extent of the Soviet's empire was the cause of its destruction.

It collapsed under its own weight.

The Weight of the World

The cost of America's elective wars is almost beyond discovery. The Pentagon estimated in 2017 that it had spent about $1.5 trillion on post-9/11 conflicts. (How it would presume to know is a puzzle, seeing as the Defense Department can't pass an audit. The first in its history, completed in 2018, was a $400 million misadventure involving 1,200 auditors. "We failed the audit, but we never expected to pass it," said deputy secretary of defense Patrick Shanahan.) Not surprisingly, the Pentagon's figures aren't even close to the real costs, according to the Watson Institute for International and Public Affairs at Brown University. It puts the total cost of post-9/11 conflicts at $6.4 trillion, or $19,560 for every man, woman, and child in America. (Here are some other metrics from their study: 801,000 people died in the violence of these wars, several times that in indirect deaths; the fighting has cost 335,000 civilians their lives; the wars have displaced or made refugees of 21 million people.)

As the Watson Institute reports, there is more to the monetary costs than just "the pointy end of the spear…. There all these other costs behind the spear." *Newsweek* provided this explanation for an earlier version of the report: "The study examines not only the money spent by the Pentagon but also the State Department, the Department of Veterans Affairs and the Department of Homeland Security, for resources dedicated to the 'war on terrorism.' The total costs include financial support for allies in the battle against extremist groups, mostly from eastern Europe, such as Croatia, Georgia, Hungary, Poland, and Romania, and a trillion dollars added for the care of veterans who may have received injuries in the conflicts."

Because, as it notes, the wars in Iraq, Afghanistan, Pakistan, and Syria, unlike prior wars, have been paid for mostly by borrowing, the report includes the interest expense already paid on these wars. It does not include future interest expense. "Even if the US stopped spending money on these wars right now," says the report, "cumulated interest costs on borrowing ultimately will add more than $7.9 trillion to the national debt over the next several decades."

Certainly, the cost of being the American Global Military Empire, which means the total cost of the national security state since the Empire has to maintain at least seventeen intelligence, spy, and surveillance agencies, not to mention plying foreign satraps with cash and hardware, paying retirement and other benefits for veterans, and its share of the national debt, is substantially more than $1 trillion annually. And it has been that high for years.

The Endgame

Will the American Global Military Empire end with a whimper or with a bang?

As the clouds of the coronavirus pandemic gathered, thick with the dark threat of a global depression, and accompanied by the rolling thunder of central banks around the world running their money-printing presses at high speed, some wondered if the storm would be enough to end the US empire.

Expecting "a hard reckoning for the allocation of our diminished resources," Pat Buchanan asked if the pandemic would prove to be "the decisive factor in America's retreat from global hegemony."

"Policing the planet is likely to be seen as yesterday's priority," he said.

But a common threat to humanity notwithstanding, there was no sign of a change in priorities. Even as the pandemic spread in 2020 (and while American cities burned and looters ran wild), the US continued pushing regime change in Iran and Venezuela. Despite some public relations posturing to the contrary, the US cranked up its maximum pressure campaign on Iran and substantially built up its naval presence in the Caribbean near Venezuela.

In May, when Iran sent five oil tankers carrying 60 million gallons of much needed gasoline to Venezuela in exchange for Venezuelan gold, the Trump administration pronounced itself "not pleased." The *Washington Post* reported that a senior official said the administration "would not abide" Iran's support of Maduro.

The Trump administration was "taking a kind of 'kick them while they're down' approach," according to a former State Department sanctions official. Its hope, he said, was "that by piling on sanctions and other actions, the administration can capitalize on the virus in Iran and Venezuela to spur greater public opposition to the incumbent governments and perhaps regime change."

Will the Deep State in any presidency persist in maintaining an interventionist presence around the globe until it crumbles into the ashes of currency destruction and bankruptcy? Although sustained by borrowing from abroad, presidents of both parties have wasted no time escalating overseas military operations and insisting on ever more spending on military might. Will the Empire simply exhaust itself financially, as it reacts desperately to its declining power and influence, spending its remaining credit and finally finishing off its currency in an effort to maintain a pretense of global power?

Or will it "busy giddy minds with foreign wars," diverting the people's attention from its manifest incompetence and the fraying of our social fabric domestically, to win the enthusiasm of the chest-thumpers? Many people wondered aloud if the first Trump war would be with China, Russia, or Iran. Trump certainly showed himself to be uncommonly interested in wielding deadly power. He repeatedly pressed a foreign policy adviser during the 2016 campaign to explain why the US can't use its nuclear weapons, and after election immediately jumped on board the $1.7 trillion nuclear weapons modernization program.

Will the Empire's hubris set off a chain reaction that results in illuminating the earth's skies with a blinding flash?

Neither outcome—the whimpering end of a painful bankruptcy or a conflict with the potential bang of a nuclear finale—is to be hoped for. Both are an affront to America's founding ideals that envisioned a prosperous people managing their own affairs secured in the blessings of liberty.

Both are endgames for a global Empire that should never have been. When empires fail, so too does their money. The dollar is coextensive with the Empire. They will fall as one.

But gold—the preferred money of the ages—will remain standing.

THE MALEVOLENT CONVERGENCE—AND YOUR ACTION PLAN

If you had known in the summer of 1976, when gold was only about one hundred dollars an ounce and silver was just over four dollars, that Jimmy Carter would be elected president a few weeks later, that he would spike the national debt by 43 percent, and that a few years into his presidency the inflation rate would hit double digits, you might very well have invested in gold.

If you had known then its monetary policies were so daft that the Federal Reserve would change interest rates twenty-three times in 1978 alone, you surely would have invested in precious metals.

But what if you had foreseen the other events that converged just three years after Carter's election? That in November 1979, a group of Iranian students would seize the US embassy in Tehran and take sixty-three American hostages, and that Iran's foreign accounts would be frozen by the United States. And what if you had known that those events would be followed within weeks by the Soviet invasion of Afghanistan? That the

Soviets, who seemed to be on the march around the world that fall, including in the Western Hemisphere, would establish diplomatic relations with the new leftist Sandinista regime in Nicaragua and would soon provide the Sandinistas with free armaments including attack helicopters, even as a coup had ignited a civil war in nearby El Salvador. With all that going on in the fall of 1979, what if you had had also foreseen that a handful of Islamic fundamentalist gunmen would take over the Great Mosque in Mecca?

You would have done very well indeed buying gold and silver before they raced to new all-time highs of $850 and $50 an ounce, respectively.

Just as one might have foreseen the fiscal and monetary pressures building in the Carter years, one might have seen the debt exploding in the Bush years, or the Fed's new quantitative easing that started at the time of Obama's election. If so, the bull market that rocketed gold to $1,900 in 2011 would have been foreseeable.

As we have carefully described in Part One of this book, today's fiscal and monetary malfeasance dwarf both of those episodes.

But as you have discovered in reading *The Last Gold Rush… Ever!*, we have gone beyond the Federal Reserve's monetary malfeasance and Washington's metastasizing federal debt. In Part Two, we have drawn on decades of our combined professional experience with vantage points that have allowed us to spot other developments that threaten to have a major impact on the markets, the dollar, and our economy. It has been our intention to share with you our conclusions, that we are approaching the malevolent convergence of economic events that will rock America to it foundations:

- trade and currency wars that will make the world poorer and that no one can win;

- a war on cash that will reveal the desperation of the dollar's manipulators and drive more people to monetary alternatives;

- a hard ending of the old-world order of American global economic and geopolitical dominance;

- the acceleration of banana republic and socialist governance at home and their ruinous indifference to fiscal probity;

- and the overstretch and ending, quietly or violently, of America's Global Military Empire.

Certainly there are other possibilities that we have not discussed, however exceedingly remote they may be. An asteroid could strike the earth, throwing civilization back into a new dark age. Or the government could suddenly embark on a path of fiscal and monetary responsibility.

But we thought it better to limit this book to likely possibilities.

We deem each of the "accelerants" described herein as real possibilities because each is already underway. Each is casting a shadow before itself. And each is capable of fueling the runaway gold and silver markets already made certain by the coming monetary and debt crises.

It is, of course, impossible to know when and how much each of these accelerants will add, but they mutually reinforce one another, and in almost any combination the conflagration will be enough to end the role of the fiat dollar as we know it.

We are not alone in making this bold forecast. Our friend, former congressman and presidential candidate Ron Paul, has substantial credibility in these issues since he too foresaw the prior crises. In a 2017 year-end interview, Dr. Paul said, "We're on the verge of something like what happened in 1989 when the Soviet system just collapsed. I'm just hoping our system comes apart as gracefully as the Soviet system."

We would have to be very lucky indeed, in our opinion, for events to change with as little upheaval.

Your Action Plan

Owning physical gold and silver must be your first step preserving your wealth and protecting yourself and your family in *The Last Gold Rush…Ever.*

We want you to beat the rush.

With so many opportunities to invest in precious metals in so many ways—in offshore accounts, ETFs, stocks, and commodity and leveraged accounts—let us be clear that we are not recommending any of these vehicles.

The mismanagement of the dollar is not the only risk we face today. There are institutional risks associated with unallocated accounts, depositories, banks, insurance companies, brokerage houses, stock and commodity exchanges, and money managers.

And there are credit and counterparty risks. Among those are the risks of nonpayment, as well as default and bankruptcy by individuals and entities who are party to a loan, contract, or investment in which you have an interest.

Wobbly and unsound financial institutions are the first to succumb to economic turmoil. The economic fallout from the pandemic shutdown will last for years; it will be felt in unexpected places. In the words of Warren Buffett, it's only when the tide goes out that you discover who's been swimming naked.

Gold and silver are the only monetary assets that are not someone else's liability. They are not dependent on the solvency or even the integrity of an issuer or counterparty.

When buyers have fled and bids are not to be found for other assets, from real estate to mortgage securities to sovereign debt instruments; when funds blow up; when money managers commit fraud; when counterparty risk and insolvent nations and mismanaged banks make everything else illiquid; physical gold remains liquid. It is the de facto reserve currency of the world.

But that is *only true* for those who own physical gold and silver that they can get their hands on when they wish. That means not relying on paper gold instruments and gold proxies. Only tangible precious metals under your own control can insulate you from dangerously unacceptable levels of governmental and institutional risk.

There are wise ways to invest in gold and silver, the world money *par excellence.* But there are pitfalls as well.

To invest wisely and avoid pitfalls, we recommend you invest in gold and silver bullion products. That means coins and bars that sell based on their actual precious metals content, and as we will explain, not numismatic coins, so-called "collectibles," marketed for their rarity.

Gold

There are two forms of gold bullion: coins and bars. In the United States, gold bullion coins are much more popular than gold bars. The most popular one-ounce gold coin is the US Mint's American Gold Eagle. The second most widely traded gold coin is the South African Krugerrand, followed by the Royal Canadian Mint's Maple Leaf, Australia's Perth Mint Kangaroo, and Austria's Philharmonic.

Gold Eagles and Krugerrands are 91.67 percent (twenty-two karat) gold, since they contain some alloy for minting purposes, while the Maple Leafs, Kangaroos, and Philharmonics are pure gold. Nevertheless, each of these contains one ounce of actual gold.

All coins and bar have premiums, prices over the benchmark or "spot price of gold." Those premiums represent minting, distribution, and other costs over the world gold price, just as a quart of motor oil is not just a quart's fractional share of the world price of a barrel of oil.

Each of these bullion coins sells at nearly the same premium, although because of their popularity, Gold Eagles generally carry slightly higher premiums.

In normal market conditions, Gold Eagles carry premiums of 3.5 to 4.5 percent over the value of their gold content; Krugerrands, the Canadian Maple Leaf coins, Kangaroos, and Philharmonics can be purchased at slightly lower premiums. In more active markets, premiums often rise.

Gold bullion coins are produced by government mints, while many gold bullion bars are produced by private mints. The best known of these in the US is PAMP, a leading Swiss refinery. PAMP also produces the popular Credit Suisse gold bars. However, some government mints, such as the Royal Canadian Mint and the Perth Mint, also produce gold bullion bars.

Gold bars sell at lower premiums than gold coins, and larger bars sell at still lower premiums than smaller bars. As an example, kilo bars (32.15 ounces) carry the lowest premiums, about 1.3 percent in normal market conditions. As the bars get smaller, the premiums rise. One-ounce bars have premiums of about 2.25 percent.

Which forms of gold are right for you depends on how much you plan to invest and the size of your portfolio. Because of their lower premiums, kilo gold bars give you more metal for the money and can be most suitable for those investing hundreds of thousands or even millions of dollars. Yet others investing millions in gold still prefer to own one-ounce coins like the Gold Eagle or Gold Maple Leaf, coins that are well-suited for smaller investors as well.

In an environment of serious economic problems, one-ounce gold coins can be convenient to trade for products or services that you may need. In severe circumstances, smaller, fractional-ounce coins make sense, but only if you can acquire them at low premiums.

Choosing Silver

Silver coins are highly recommended for a monetary crisis for several reasons. Pre-1965 US 90 percent silver coins, dimes, quarters, and half-dollars (commonly called "junk silver coins" because they have no collector value) were minted to be used as money. They can be used as money again in a worst-case scenario. These coins are valued and priced based on their silver content, not their face value. Dimes and quarters are generally readily available; at times, half-dollars can become scarce.

For investors who think that in the future they will simply sell their silver and return to dollars, 100-ounce silver bars can be a good choice because they are easier to handle and store. Still, 90 percent silver coins remain popular with investors. However, it takes more space to store the bags of 90 percent silver coins as it does the compact 100-ounce silver bars. At times, silver bars carry slightly higher premiums than pre-1965 silver coins. In active markets, the coins can carry premiums of several dollars an ounce over 100-ounce silver bars.

A hugely popular silver product is the US Mint's one-ounce American Silver Eagle coin. Although they carry premiums of $2.75 to $3 each, more than 400 million Silver Eagles have been sold. Other popular silver products are ten-ounce bars and privately minted one-ounce silver rounds.

What Not to Buy

When investing in gold and silver, it's important to know what not to buy. At times, all forms of gold and silver liquidate at the same price; therefore, you should avoid buying high-premium items. Proof Gold Eagles and old US gold coins are excellent examples of what not to buy, as well as other high-premium gold coins that are regularly promoted.

The US Mint sells Proof Gold Eagles today at more than $300 per ounce over the spot or benchmark gold price. Yet in the period from 2017 to 2019, they liquidated at or near 1 percent over spot, the same as bullion Gold Eagles.

Old US gold coins have been promoted since the 1980s by telemarketers as the best way to own gold. An analysis of their price history does not support this position.

Because they have been promoted for so long, they generally had "natural premiums" of 20 percent to 30 percent over their gold content, and sometimes higher. But then, telemarketers often tack on an additional 30 percent to 50 percent or more when selling them.

During 2017 through 2019, premiums on old US gold coins shrank to just about the level of bullion coin premiums, and those that had been persuaded, often by high-pressure and specious sales representations, to invest in these high-mark-up products suffered huge losses. Often, they experienced these losses although the underlying price of gold itself had risen.

At times, old US gold coins sell at or near the same low premiums found on bullion coins. Then they can be an advantageous investment because their premiums may return. If not, they remain gold coins with low premiums.

Gold or Silver?

In past precious metals bull markets, silver has turned in higher percentage gains than gold. The prime example is the 1971 to 1980 period. Gold went from $35 to $850 for a 2,400 percent gain; however, silver turned in a 3,300 percent gain, going from $1.50 to $50.

In the 2004 to 2011 period, silver went up 6.25 times, while gold climbed four times.

However, keep in mind that silver's bulk and weight at today's relative values is about eighty times that of gold, which can make handling and storage an issue.

Both gold and silver have distinct investor applications, features that make each convenient and efficient in a variety of circumstances. All things considered, you will be delighted to own either metal or both during *The Last Gold Rush...Ever.*

INDEX

ABOUT THE AUTHORS

Charles Goyette is a *New York Times* bestselling author, commentator, and talk show host, best known for his penetrating views on markets and economic issues. He has appeared often on national TV on CNN, Fox News, MSNBC, CNBC, Fox Business, and PBS.

After receiving his degree in finance from the University of Colorado, Bill Haynes founded CMI Gold & Silver in 1973. Located in Phoenix, his company is one of the oldest dealers in the US, and has introduced precious metals to thousands of investors.